OPEN AND DISTANCE LEARNING SERIES

Key Terms and Issues

in Open and

Distance Learning

BARBARA HODGSON

KOGAN PAGE
Published in association with the
Institute of Educational Technology, Open University

London ● Philadelphia

First published in 1993

Kogan Page Limited
120 Pentonville Road
London N1 9JN

British Library Cataloguing in Publication Data

A CIP record for this book is available from the British Library

ISBN 0 7494 0710 7

Typeset by BookEns Limited, Baldock, Herts.
Printed and bound in Great Britain by Biddles Ltd, Guildford and King's Lynn.

Contents

Acknowledgements

The book has arisen out of work over many years with colleagues in the Institute of Educational Technology in the Open University, as well as colleagues throughout the university, and from other open and distance learning organizations around the world. I am particularly grateful to Brendan Connors for his wide expertise, and for specific contributions from Fiona Butcher, Brenda Crouch, Nicola Durbridge, Gerald Hales, Roger Harrison, David Hawkridge, Jane Henry, Tony Kaye, Clive Lawless, Fred Lockwood, Robin Mason, Reg Melton, Judith Riley, Bernadette Robinson, Derek Rowntree, Eileen Scanlon, Rob Waller, Alan Woodley and Bob Zimmer.

Grateful acknowledgement is due to the Open University for permission to reproduce Figures 2, 3, 4, 5 and 7 and for the material that makes up Figure 8 and to Kogan Page for Figures 1 and 9.

Series editor's foreword

The use of open and distance learning is increasing dramatically in all sections of education and training, both in the UK and around the world. Many schools, colleges, universities, companies and organizations are already using open and distance learning practices in their teaching and training and want to develop these further. Furthermore, many individuals have heard about open and distance learning and would welcome the opportunity to find out more about it and explore its potential.

Whatever your current interest in open and distance learning and experience within it, I believe there will be something in this series of short books for you. This series is directed at teachers, trainers, educational advisers, in-house training managers and training consultants involved in designing open and distance learning systems and materials. It will be invaluable for those working in learning environments ranging from industry and commerce to public sector organizations, from schools and colleges to universities.

This series is designed to provide a comprehensive coverage of the field of open and distance learning. Each title focuses on a different aspect of designing and developing open and distance learning and provides concrete advice and information, which is built upon current theory and research in the field and how it relates to actual practice. This basis, of theory, research and development experience, is unique in the area of open and distance learning. I say this with some confidence since the Open University Institute of Educational Technology, from which virtually all the authors are drawn, contains the largest collection of educational technologists (course designers, developers and researchers) in the world. Since the inception of the Open University in 1969 members of the Institute have made a major contribution to the design and production of learning systems and materials, not just in the Open University, but in many other organizations in the UK and many countries around the world. We would now like to share our experience and findings with you.

For those venturing into the field of open and distance learning, the prospect can be daunting: a whole new array of issues and concepts, terms and phrases used by the initiated. This glossary should allay such fears. In a simple and direct way, Barbara Hodgson identifies, explains and illustrates those issues that are at the centre of open and distance learning today. Other concepts, words and phrases in widespread use, both within open and distance learning and teaching and training generally, are also explained with clear cross-reference to other entries. The author also begins to unravel the phrases 'open learning' and 'distance learning' as well as putting current developments into an international context. Those who merely want to dip into the book from time to time, and others who want to readily explore the current ideas in an effective and efficient way, will find this book invaluable.

Fred Lockwood

Introduction

Open learning – distance learning?

What do people mean when they talk about open learning or distance learning? The terms are obviously not synonymous or we would not need to use both in discussion in teaching and training, in the professional and research literature, or indeed in the title of this book and its series. Equally, open and distance learning must have much in common or the terms would not be linked together as they so frequently are.

Both open learning and distance learning are terms that have been in common use in education and training circles over the last 20 years, along with close relatives such as flexible learning, flexistudy, supported self-study, resource-based learning and so on. It is difficult, though, to find succinct and complete definitions of either term as both are interpreted and practised differently according to need and circumstance. This leads to a perennial need to qualify or extend a definition for a particular purpose and has given rise to an ongoing academic/semantic debate as you will see if you browse through journals such as *Open Learning* (itself originally called *Teaching at a Distance*) and *Distance Education*. Here are just a few definitions or descriptions of open learning:

> . . . a process which focuses on access to educational opportunities and a philosophy which makes learning more client and student centred. It is learning which allows the learner to choose *how* to learn, *when* to learn, *where* to learn and *what* to learn as far as possible within the constraints of any education and training provision (Paine, 1989, p. ix).

> Open learning is a term used to describe courses flexibly designed to meet individual requirements. It is often applied to provision which tries to remove barriers that prevent attendance at more traditional courses, but it also suggests a learner-centred philosophy (Lewis and Spencer, 1986, p. 9).

> . . . one could not nail Open Learning to the floor as a fixed concept. It was, and continues to be, a process (Coffey, 1988, p.195).

Open learning is a state of mind rather than a method with particular characteristics (Jack, 1988, p.52).

Open learning is a multi-faceted concept. Open learning attempts to reduce, if not eliminate, a number of barriers which either stop or impede certain groups of students from participating in formal education. Open learning also attempts to provide a learning environment which will provide these groups of students, on entering various courses of study, with the best possible chance of successfully completing the learning experiences they have chosen (Holt and Bonnici, 1988, p.245).

and of distance learning (or distance education as it is also often called):

In distance education, the learner and the teacher are not face-to-face. In order for two-way communication to take place between them, a medium such as print, radio or the telephone has to be used (Perry and Rumble, 1987, p.1).

Distance education, in contrast to traditional classroom or campus based education, is characterised by a clear separation in space and time of the majority of teaching and learning activities. Teaching is to a large degree mediated through various technologies (print, audio, video, broadcasting, computers), and learning generally takes place on an individual basis through supported independent study in the student's home or workplace (Kaye, 1989, p.6).

Distance education is a form of education characterised by

- the quasi-permanent separation of the teacher and learner throughout the length of the learning process;
- the influence of an educational organisation both in the planning and preparation of learning materials and in the provision of student support services;
- the use of technical media – print, audio, video or computer – to unite teacher and learner and carry the content of the course;
- the provision of two-way communication so that the student may benefit from or even initiate dialogue; and
- the quasi-permanent absence of the learning group throughout the length of the learning process so that people are usually taught as individuals and not in groups, with the possibility of occasional meetings for both didactic and socialisation purposes (Keegan, 1990, p.44).

You will notice that descriptions of open learning emphasize that it is a process and draw attention to the benefits to learners. The definitions of distance learning focus on the process and give an indication of the ways in which it works. Many people see the distinction between them in this way. Open learning is an educational philosophy; distance learning is an educational delivery system to meet particular needs.

Most systems, whichever way they are designated, have elements of both openness and distance. Confusion or blurring often arises because of the names that institutions or organizations adopt. The Open University in the UK is a good example. A distance teaching university in its mode of delivery of learning, it has very much as its *raison d'être* the provision of flexible, learner-centred learning opportunities with open access to learners who would not otherwise be able to study at university level. But it also offers a variety of other learning opportunities and the degree of openness varies. Similarly with Indira Ghandi National Open University in India. Some other 'distance' teaching universities use the word distance in their titles – for example, Universidad Nacional de Educación a Distancia in Spain – and perhaps openness is less of an issue. Something like the ICI Open Learning Centre may be relatively open to employees of ICI but does not have the general openness of, say, an Open College course or one from the National Extension College, an organization which has neither 'open' nor 'distance' in its title but is, in fact, both. As you explore different interpretations of openness and practices of distance you will find, as Rowntree (1992) concludes:

> All open learning (even on-site) involves a degree of distance. Not all distance learning involves much openness – except perhaps of time, place or pace. But many so-called open learning systems don't involve much of any other kind of openness either. And some learning systems that don't call themselves open are actually more open than some that do (p. 32).

Why open and distance learning?

Providers of education and training move into open and distance learning for a variety of reasons. It may be to offer a particular opportunity, such as a professional training, to a much wider audience of learners or to offer a much wider choice of learning opportunities to a particular audience, such as a workforce. Sometimes it is in an attempt to reduce education or training costs both in terms of money and time. Or it may be to make a system more cost-effective by reaching a bigger market. Often it is in an attempt to produce education or training for individuals as and when they need it rather than them having to wait for a viable group to work with. Usually it is to some extent in the spirit of the philosophy, outlined earlier, of providing access to opportunities which are flexible enough to meet an individual's requirements and sufficiently well designed to assure a reasonable chance of success.

Sometimes national need is the driving force. Distance learning has provided the answer for secondary and higher education systems which cannot cope with the speed and scale of necessary expansion in conventional ways; the Open Secondary School in Indonesia is a good example of this. Developing countries, including Zimbabwe, Guyana, Bangladesh, Sri Lanka, Nigeria, Cameroon and Kenya, have frequently turned to distance learning to alleviate chronic shortages of trained teachers. Central and eastern European countries are currently adopting distance learning to promote the rapid and widespread introduction of western management education. Equally, distance learning can meet the needs of a sparse and geographically widespread learning community such as schoolchildren in northern Scandinavia.

The varieties and possibilities are many and fascinating. In the space of two weeks recently I have had discussions with academics from Bangladesh and from Slovakia, both about to set up Open Universities; education officials from Egypt looking to establish a large-scale programme of distance in-service education for teachers; police training officers developing a variety of open learning packages to enhance training for police officers; a representative of the United Nations High Commission for Refugees wanting to promote training, through open learning, in interviewing for refugee status; someone from a professional institute of public administration looking to offer all its qualification courses at a distance; and a group concerned with the Europe-wide provision of open learning materials for traveller education.

What is involved in open and distance learning?

In order to get started – and therefore for the purposes of this book – perhaps we need to ask not 'what is open and distance learning?', but 'how does open and distance learning work?' How do you do it ? How do you design flexible courses, eliminate barriers, provide learning environments that allow every chance of success? Answers to these sorts of questions highlight those things that open and distance learning have in common, and the things on which this book will concentrate.

All successful open and distance learning systems are built on:

• well-designed, learner-centred, self-instructional materials delivered through a variety of media and appropriate to the circumstances;

- an administrative system for distributing the materials, for keeping track of the learners and possibly a production facility for materials;
- a support system for learners.

Planners, managers, teachers and trainers in open and distance learning need to consider a wide variety of issues when planning and implementing their systems and materials. Many of these issues are not necessarily different from those of other educational or training systems but openness and distance bring special needs, problems and opportunities that must be thought about.

Issues such as: who the learners will be; what special characteristics they might have which will influence the design of the materials or support system; whether they will be able to reach particular goals from their starting points and what additional help they might need; what the learning materials should include.

Questions such as: what will the materials look like? How can learning materials be designed to be interactive? What teaching strategies will be employed and can everything be taught through open and distance learning?

Decisions need to be made about media to be used to deliver the message. What is appropriate and what is possible? What support will learners be offered and who will be responsible for this? Will learners be looking for accreditation and how will this be carried out? Will it be related to professional or national qualifications?

There are resource implications to be considered and quite possibly staff development to think about. Colleagues perhaps need to be convinced that open and distance learning is a sound and viable approach to the education or training they are charged with providing. Writers of material will need guidance and support staff will need their role defining.

If open and distance learning is to be provided on a large scale the amount of organization is considerable and many people with a wide variety of skills will contribute. But it does not have to be large scale. Individuals or small groups of teachers or trainers have successfully delivered their teaching in open learning mode with quite modest resources. They have just needed to consider all these issues for themselves and develop the appropriate skills!

How to use this book

This book addresses open and distance learning through a glossary of important issues and commonly used terms. These terms and issues are defined, described or discussed, as appropriate. Many are part of the language of teaching and learning generally, but have a particular slant or significance in open and distance learning. The book is intended as a practitioner's reference and, wherever possible, I have tried to offer readily accessible practical advice and guidance rather than just definitions.

The terms and issues selected for inclusion appear as cross-headings in **bold** and are listed alphabetically. 'Issues' are discussed at length, in perhaps a couple of pages, while 'terms' have much shorter entries, although a clear distinction is sometimes hard to maintain. I have aimed to include as many cross-references (***bold italic***) as possible, but each entry should be comprehensible on its own (giving rise to a certain amount of overlap between entries). Cross-references are also given at the end of entries where 'see also . . .' refers you to related terms and entries with additional discussion. Following entries where no definition is given, 'see . . .' refers you to related, synonymous terms.

To give an example, you may need to think about media choice in open and distance learning. The discussion under the entry for media choice will lead you also to definitions and discussion of the roles of various media such as audio, video, tutorial support, and then into thinking about production, presentation, delivery and support. Starting with the issues of presentation or style of learning materials could lead you on to teaching styles, devices for supporting learners through the design of the materials and to assessment issues. You may just want to find out what people mean when they talk about access devices or find out what a transformer is. Wherever you start, and for whatever purpose, I hope the cross-referencing will give an indication of the interdependence of all aspects of open and distance learning systems. We do need a broad perspective and understanding of the whole even if our responsibility is only for one particular element.

The glossary is not exhaustive. I have chosen to put the emphasis on self-instructional materials delivered through a variety of media and on delivery

and support systems. Where there are differences between open and distance learning, the distance learning aspects are emphasized. This is a fast-
developing field so I have also chosen to concentrate on well-established
practice. There are many current buzz words, especially in new technology
and media, where potential is seen or imagined but which may fail to work
out, prove to be too expensive for most education systems, or be superseded
and never enter the permanent vocabulary.

As it is in glossary form, this book is meant to be consulted or dipped into
as a practical reference rather than read from start to finish. Because of the
density of information, and for reasons of space, its layout does not perhaps
conform to all the best design practice of open and distance learning materials.
But of course a glossary is only one possible element of self-instructional
material, a particular access device, and I hope this one will provide access to the
design and support of successful self-instructional materials.

A

access devices make the content and structure of a learning text (and indeed any other medium of presentation) more accessible to learners studying on their own. They help the active learner to locate concepts and statements in any part of the material so as to compare or combine them with those the learner happens to be studying at any one time. Access devices can also help individual learners to approach the same material with different purposes on different occasions – to preview, to skim-read, to use for *revision,* to refer to for a specific point, etc.

These are some of the more important access devices and their functions:

Contents lists enable learners to find particular sections of the material and also provide an overview of its structure. The headings included in a contents list should work together to provide a coherent overview of the material – avoiding cryptic, whimsical or jargon-ridden headings whose meaning is only apparent when the material has been studied.

A **summary** performs as an access device when it includes the main points of one particular section. At the beginning, it acts as an *overview* without assuming familiarity with new terminology; at the end, it *reviews* the main points, concepts and conclusions. (See *summaries, objectives*.)

The *index* lists, in alphabetical order, various items discussed in the material, with their page (or other) references. Ideas, concepts and themes can be listed, as well as people, places, events and technical terms.

A *glossary* is similar. It lists and explains technical terms in alphabetical order, perhaps with their definitions. It is mainly useful as a revision aid or to remind learners of definitions they have read earlier in the text. Since the definition of many terms builds on previously defined terms, a glossary should not be considered as a substitute for the proper introduction of new words and concepts in the main text.

Within the body of the teaching material:

Headings enable learners to scan a text for items of interest, or can be used in connection with the contents list to locate specific sections. They are one of the most important access devices.

Cross-references, which may be highlighted in bold type, or set apart in a margin, or in a special box, etc., draw attention to other parts of the materials which relate to what is being studied.

Advance organizers are items which may be included at the beginning of a piece of learning material such as aims, lists of objectives, overviews and even *pre-tests*. They help to make certain aspects of the material explicable and accessible. Because texts are necessarily linear in structure, some people find it useful to add an overview in diagrammatic form (a network or flow diagram, for example) to illustrate complex non-linear relationships between the concepts discussed.

A **concept structure diagram** is often regarded as an essential step in planning teaching material. It can also be, along with *aims* and *objectives*, a considerable aid to communication among a team of teachers or writers preparing related parts of a course or material.

access material see *remedial material*.

activities, sometimes called *self-assessment* questions (SAQs), *in-text questions* (ITQs) or adjunct aids, are things you can ask learners to do, other than passively reading, watching, or listening to whatever materials are provided. They are questions or tasks designed to help learners think for themselves, come up with explanations/solutions, sort out the features of an argument, draw inferences, engage in controversy and relate their own ideas and experience to a topic. They provide opportunities for learners to be exposed to competing ideas and views, experience those tasks that are typical of the subject, practise important objectives, monitor their progress, check their understanding and reflect on implications of their learning. In essence their role is to encourage learners to actively use the material.

Devising activities is not always easy, although some teachers and writers of self-instructional material believe that activities should be the starting point. Many advise that you should devise these activities and then construct the teaching around them.

Of course pitching activities at the right level of difficulty is important. If you make them too trivial they will not help the learner, and if they are too difficult someone working alone may get stuck, needlessly discouraged, and may be tempted to *drop out*. *Developmental testing* may give you some idea about the level and effectiveness of the activities.

In order to be an effective teaching strategy in your materials, activities should include several features. For each activity you should include some contextualization of the activity within the learning and a rationale for doing it; clear instructions, with perhaps an indication or example of the expected outcome; an estimate of the amount of time you expect learners to spend on it; and, if appropriate, a space or grid in which learners can note their responses is often helpful. Most importantly, all activities need *feedback* or follow-up comments. Effective activities usually occur fairly regularly throughout a self-instructional text, probably related to each key concept or skill, and call for the practice of a wide variety of cognitive skills. It helps to have them typographically delineated in some way, perhaps boxed or indicated by a marginal *icon*. These features are illustrated in Figure 1.

advance organizers are built into the beginning of a piece of self-instructional material to give learners a general idea of what is to follow and to help organize their learning. They can take a variety of forms and be called by a number of names. A *contents list*, a *summary* – in words or diagrammatic form – of what has already been studied and how this new material relates to it, an *overview* of practical activities, eg 'this next section will involve you in . . .', or a statement of *aims* and *objectives* can all be used by the learner as advance organizers, whether or not that was the primary reason for their inclusion. Any section of learning materials labelled 'introduction' or 'overview' is usually an advance organizer.

aims are statements, couched in fairly general terms, of what the teacher or trainer intends to do during a course, a module or a lesson; they may sometimes be a broad description of what the learner is going to do. For example, in a foreign language course an important aim may be to explain and illustrate the grammatical rules governing the future tense and to practise it.

Aims are usually concerned with what the *teacher* is going to do during the course or lesson; the learner's activities if any are not often explicitly mentioned. They may express a teacher's intentions, but are far from a precise specification of what is going to take place. They are more like an architect's preliminary sketches than the detailed plans from which a building could be constructed. Although the learning experience is presumably intended to lead to some desirable outcome, aims rarely make any explicit reference to this.

Aims can communicate to prospective learners the purpose of the course and in broad terms what they might gain by studying it. They also serve as an important planning tool; where a group of people are in the first stages of designing a whole course, for example, the discussion and refining of aims may be a useful approach to early course design. However as you begin to concern yourself with the details of what is actually going to take place, a more precise form of description is needed. Learners need to know precisely what they have to do, both during and after the lesson or course. In open and distance learning you will probably also need to describe your teaching

Figure 1   *Features of effective activities (from Lockwood, 1992)*   *CONTEXT*

Writers' assumptions and expectations

SUBHEADING

TYPOGRAPHICAL TITLE

ACTIVITY 3.1 Writers' assumptions and expectations

TIME
RATIONALE

At this point I think you would find it useful to spend a couple of minutes trying to identify the assumptions that lie behind the self-instructional material that you currently assemble or are likely to assemble in the near future. In the space below you can note your main assumptions and alongside each of these you could note what your expectations are regarding the way in which your learners will study your material in general and the activities in particular.

INSTRUCTIONS

(a) What assumptions lie behind the self-instructional materials you will be assembling and the activities you will be devising?

(b) What expectations do you have regarding the way in which learners will study your material in general and the activities in particular ?

Example:

ASSUMPTION
1. Activities are an integral part of teaching, a way to realize key objectives, with the rest of the material built around them.

EXPECTATION
Learners will recognize the central place of activities in their study since they provide an opportunity to realize and practise objectives.

EXAMPLE

2.

SPACE OR GRID

3.

4.

FEEDBACK

So what assumptions, and corresponding expectations, regarding activities and learner use did you identify? I obviously can't know which ones you have listed but I can share with you those listed by other teachers and writers. In surveys of OU authors and discussion with other writers of self-instructional material five major ones have emerged; I've summarized these in Figure 3.1. As I go through them perhaps you would like to consider how they compare with yours and whether you would adopt or reject them.

and learning processes accurately to other teachers or trainers; learning materials are usually mediated and often assessed by someone other than the writer so your intended learning paths and outcomes must be explicit. For this sort of intercommunication between teacher, learners and other teachers a simple statement of aims is not enough. A few examples of the kind of test question or situation which learners will be expected to answer or handle, or a set of *objectives* are needed.

assessment is the measurement of aspects of a learner's performance in terms of knowledge, skills and attitudes (usually referred to as 'evaluation' in the USA). It is necessary in that both teachers and learners need *feedback* and because society (including the learners) usually expects some provision of a summary of what people know and can do. In open and distance learning, assessment has many dimensions. It can be formal or informal, carried out by the learners themselves, by tutors or computers. It can be *formative* or *summative*. It may be immediate or delayed, paper- or computer-based, or on-the-job assessment. (See also *competence, continuous assessment, criterion-referenced assessment, examinations, norm-referenced assessment, objective tests, self-assessment*.)

assignments can be any piece of work that a learner is required to complete for assessment. It may be an exercise that is part of the learning process but more usually it means a piece of work submitted by a learner to a tutor for *feedback* and *marking* and possibly grading in order to fulfil the requirement for the award of a qualification. Many forms of teaching use assignments, but they are particularly important in self-instructional systems, where they perform a number of different functions. They help to ensure that learners actually do the necessary work, that they keep up to date, and that they achieve a satisfactory standard. They provide an essential element of practice and may help learners to check their own understanding and competence. Also, they may be used to control progression to the next stage of the course.

Since distance learners usually have no one to turn to for clarification, the precise wording of assignments is crucial. Instructions to the learner must be clear and unambiguous. They should cover the type and length of response expected, the time you expect them to take over it, and the time and place of handing in. Make sure, perhaps by *developmental testing*, that the assignment can be answered by users of your material, and that it cannot be interpreted in several different ways. Learners have been known to waste many hours attempting faulty assignments.

audio In multimedia learning packages the word 'audio' includes radio, records, compact discs, audio cassettes, etc. Except for cassettes, these may be too complicated and expensive for you to consider when preparing your own learning materials. Nevertheless it may be possible to make use of an existing radio programme or recording, and it is always worth investigating such a possibility before you get involved with making your own audio component(s). Remember, though, that actually incorporating ready-made professional material as part of your own materials may introduce *copyright* complications, and copyright fees can be expensive.

Audio cassettes are a cheap and convenient way in which you can add an audio component to a learning package and, except perhaps for music and language courses, their quality of reproduction is usually quite adequate. They can help to convey a sense of 'dialogue' so that, in addition to their teaching function, they can help to bring teacher and learner closer together. The spoken word has advantages over the printed text because it can give the listener audible clues about how to interpret and evaluate the message. Pitch, pace, tone and inflexion add meaning to the spoken word. By varying these you can achieve variety, conveying your enthusiasm for your subject and motivating your learners.

Another useful characteristic of audio cassettes is that learners can do more than just listen; using the pause, rewind and fast-forward facilities, equivalent to *access devices* in text, they can organize and reorganize their own experience of the content. Learners can pick their own times and points on the tape to start and stop, skimming and revising at will.

Cassettes are also very flexible from the teacher's point of view. You can choose from a range of strategies with many imaginative variations depending on the subject matter and skills involved. For example, by providing *material for simple listening* you can raise learners' awareness, add enrichment material, discuss alternatives, reduce anxiety, etc. When *listening is interspersed with activities* the learner can be asked to switch off the tape, to pause and think at intervals or perhaps attempt longer exercises. With eyes and hands free, learners can *listen and look or do simultaneously*. They can be 'talked through' such things as complex diagrams, maps, charts, tables of statistics, biological or geological specimens, as well as being 'talked through' complicated exercises, setting up equipment or doing experiments. (See *audiovision*.)

audio letter, audio tutorial You can use cassettes as part of the direct teaching strategy of your course, and for other things such as counselling, remedial teaching, or as transcription and reminder of tutorial sessions. A genuine dialogue can be developed between teacher and learner and among a learning group if, for instance, questions are recorded by the learner and sent to the tutor to record her answers. This can be cheaper than telephone calls. There are a number of applications like this which can be made useful if learners do not often meet a tutor or each other face-to-face, or if some learners are isolated from the group by perhaps distance or disability.

audiovision is a powerful technique that enables you to prompt and guide learners while they are practising some manual skill or making a close, careful and, above all, uninterrupted, visual examination of something you want them to look at.

There are many occasions when learners find themselves trying to look at several things at once. It is impossible, for example, simultaneously to read an article on international trade, look at the relevant maps, and also consult a table of export statistics. Each has to be looked at in turn, and we all know how difficult it is to find our place again in the original text whenever we stop in the middle of a page to look for a very small feature in a large and complex map, or consult the correct row and column in a table of statistics. It is equally difficult to read detailed instructions on how to perform a calculation, look at the diagram on which the calculation is based, and push the right buttons on the calculator without finding we have lost our place in the instructions, or, at the very least that our concentration on any one item has been diluted because of the need to look at the others. There are similar problems in many subject areas when complex things like diagrams, maps, tables of statistics or musical scores have to be examined closely in precise ways.

There are even more problems when learners have to use their hands as well as their eyes. If they have to hold a slide viewer, or tilt an exhibit this way and that in order to examine it in detail, they will probably have to put it down in order to turn back and read the self-instructional material that discusses what they have been looking at. If they are learning some form of manual skill they may find it very difficult to get it all together if, after practising each small detailed operation, there is a long delay while they find the next instruction.

All this need be no great problem in face-to-face teaching, because it is relatively easy for a live teacher to prompt and guide a learner in a close and uninterrupted examination of the exhibit. It need be no great problem for distant learners, either, if you recognize that an *audio* component is not only a substitute for, but in one respect at least, an actual improvement on the voice of a live teacher. What live teacher can be made at the touch of a button to repeat what he or she has just said, go back to the beginning, to jump forward in the explanation, or (often very difficult indeed) simply remain silent for a while? Audiovision is controlled by the learners. It can provide a guiding voice in their ears while their eyes are engaged in an important, prolonged and concentrated visual examination, or while their hands and eyes are practising a psychomotor skill. They may look without listening or listen without looking if they so wish and it can all be repeated as many times as each thinks necessary.

This can be done so easily that audiovision is in many respects superior to *television*, *video*, or *computer-assisted learning*, and it has all the other advantages of audio material. The voice of the teacher provides a personal link, something that is particularly valuable in open and distance education. The necessary hardware is cheaper, much more portable, and much more widely available. The software – an audio cassette – is cheap, compact, light and durable and easily distributed, by post if need be. There are unlikely to be compatibility problems and an audiotape recording is cheap to update or remake. If you have things that you want your learners to scrutinize with great care, or skills that involve coordination of hand and eye, you should exploit all the advantages that audiovision offers.

C

charts see *diagrams*, *illustrations*.

competence generally is the application of knowledge, skills and attitudes to tasks or combinations of tasks to the requisite standards under operational conditions. In terms of *vocational qualifications* competence is the ability to perform work activities to the standards required in employment. For assessment for the award of *NVQs*, competences are divided into units and subdivided into elements. An element must be stated with great precision and always requires performance criteria to indicate the standard at which the element of competence must be demonstrated. Elements of competence are thus comparable with what in other education and training systems are known as competence objectives, learning *objectives* or learning outcomes. Statements of competence will fulfil the same function as objectives when designing and writing self-instructional material for training leading to NVQs.

computer-assisted learning (CAL) There are lots of initials referring to different ways of using computers to support the learning process. There are various nuances of meaning but some mean much the same thing. Differences in meaning may be context-dependent. Computer-based learning (CBL) and computer-based training (CBT) are other commonly used expressions.

Computer-assisted learning may be described as the interactive use of computers for explicit learning purposes and there are various ways in which computers are used for this. One obvious way is for drill-and-practice as the computer can be resourceful and patient. Programs of this type range from question-and-answer series to fairly elaborate problem-solving, but they seldom give feedback to learners who make mistakes. They rely on the attention-getting power of the computer to keep learners drilling and practising particular skills, usually formal ones like arithmetical procedures, solving equations or correcting language usage, but also practically orientated skills such as the use of spreadsheets in accounting.

Learners can be more in charge of their learning through the use of simulation programs and educational games. Such programs usually aim to provide practice of skills in a motivating form and to promote exploration by the learner that will lead to discovery of general principles. At a simple level, spelling games fall into this category. At a much higher level, simulation of experiments involving the laws of physics may help learners to understand the complexity of relationships represented by sets of equations that in turn are governed by the laws of probability.

Tutorial and coaching type programs do offer feedback to the learner. The 'tutor' part of the program monitors what is happening to the learners and, depending on the mistakes they make, intervenes with advice. Simple ones offer advice when learners make the wrong choice in a multiple-choice question or contain hints that a learner can obtain through a help menu. More elaborate ones are aimed at knowing what the learners are doing, preventing them from forming grossly incorrect concepts, helping them to see the limits of their learning strategies, and guiding them to discover the causes of their errors. Self-testing can, of course, be a feature of most programs.

The problems associated with including CAL in a self-instructional package are related to cost. All learners must have access to suitable computing facilities and you have to provide appropriate software. Suitable programs may be available commercially or because you have already developed them for your teaching. If they have to be developed specially this can be time-consuming and costly and may only be cost-effective if you are teaching or training on a very large scale or if use of the computer *per se* is an important part of the training package.

computer conferencing is a way of using the transfer of text for group communication or conferencing. Learners and tutors are linked by a computer/telecommunications network to a common text-storage space for discussion, exchange and communal activity. This system offers learners in isolation the possibility of group work, of very quick feedback and interaction with peers and teachers. Communication is asynchronous so it is used at a time convenient to each participant. Learners are not obliged to respond immediately to questions and to other participants' interventions as they would be in face-to-face, telephone or live broadcast conferencing. Contributions can be read and reflected on and learners' own contributions can be added when ready and when convenient. Conference transcripts become valuable records and resources and can possibly be used as the basis of a group project or report.

computer-managed learning (CML) describes the use of a computer to manage a learning system. This could be by keeping enrolment records and learner progress records, providing test structures, guiding learners to new lessons or courses on the basis of their achievements, managing materials distribution systems, timetabling and scheduling and maybe even the production, or on-line delivery of materials.

computer-marked assignments (CMAs) The idea behind objective testing is that it is possible to ask various kinds of questions to which there is only one 'best' answer or set of answers; the familiar one-from-several multiple-choice questions are just one example of this. The learner's responses consist of a relatively small number of alternatives, so the marking can be done with no knowledge of the subject. All that is needed is a template that can be placed over a standardized answer form to reveal whether the learner's coded responses are in the right place – a mechanical process that can be automated and so is very useful with large numbers of learners.

One way is to use an optical-scanning device to recognize coded pencil-marks made by the learner and to digitize this information for computer processing. The computer can then do far more than merely mark the correct answers. It can be programmed to perform almost any kind of marking operation, to process the raw scores in some way, to record the results, to notify the learners and teachers concerned and to perform the kind of statistical analyses that seek to explore the quality of both the individual test items and the test as a whole. It can also be programmed to produce individualized *feedback* to learners based on, say, relating common errors or misconceptions to particular incorrect answers. As more and more tests take place, it can also store all the information acquired in this way and display it in various formats when required. Nor does this necessarily call for a mainframe computer; where the scale of operations is modest a micro-computer is adequate.

It is not always necessary for the learner to make a mark on a piece of paper. Where learners have easy access to computer terminals or personal computers they can log on to the system, ask for the test required, have the questions presented and key in the chosen answer directly. Also you can build up a bank of test items for each of the tests that the learner has to take, and ask the computer to make a random selection from the bank of items whenever a test is required. You can instruct it to give the learners no feed-back about the accuracy of their answers until all the learners have taken the test. Alternatively, you can program it to give immediate feedback, in which case it becomes a powerful revision, or even tutorial device for the learner who sits at the terminal. This is especially useful in distance education systems where learner and computer can be connected via a telecommunications system. Computer-marked assignments can thus be a quick and efficient way of providing learners with regular information about their progress. But to a group of learners that has few human contacts it can seem a highly impersonal, and perhaps even threatening way of doing things. For this reason, everything about a computer-marking system should be explained fully to both learners and tutors. An appeal system may be necessary too, for learners who suspect (usually baselessly) that the computer has made errors. These reservations apart, and never forgetting that any form of objective testing has its own limitations and requires teachers to learn its own special techniques, computer marking can be a very useful facility for distance learners and teachers alike.

computer-mediated communication (CMC) refers to the possibilities which exist when computers and telecommunication networks are used as tools in the communications process: to compose, store, deliver and process communication. Such systems rely on a basic configuration of a mainframe computer with appropriate software, connected via telephone and data networks to users with terminals or micro-computers. Various learning experiences can be built upon these communication processes and so they are sometimes used as a medium in open and distance learning packages.

CMC covers a range of different facilities including:

- access to remote databases such as bibliographic sources, sets of abstracts, or details of courses available;
- electronic mail, which allows messages to be sent to electronic letter boxes for named individuals, which can be accessed when the named user logs on;
- computer-conferencing, which allows messages to be shared openly by all members of a conference.

Such facilities have many uses and advantages in open and distance learning but presuppose access to expensive hardware with not inconsiderable running costs. Building a course around CMC could lead to the exclusion of many potential learners on cost grounds. Such methods of delivery may well be very successful for work-based training and can be globally available to participants.

contents lists see *access devices.*

continuous assessment The award of a qualification may depend on satisfactory performance in an end-of-course examination, or on the satisfactory completion of a set of tasks throughout the learning period, or on a combination of both. The latter is often referred to as continuous assessment, even though it may be more periodic than continuous.

Some form of continuous assessment is generally an important feature of open and distance learning systems. It provides a convenient and often necessary method of motivating and pacing learners, as well as a means of keeping a record of learner progress. Learners usually respond well to continuous assessment as it gives them credit for ongoing work, but it is important not to over-assess them. If you suspect that your learners are being tested too often, you can take the strain off them by making some of the assignments/exercises/tests *formative*, ie *marking* them and providing *feedback* to the learners, but not grading them. (See also *assessment*, *assignments*.)

Apart from such formative items, continuous assessment normally consists of a number of assignments which the learner sends in for marking and grading. If you have a completely open and flexible system, when learners choose to be assessed will be entirely up to them, within whatever organizational constraints you have to work. If there are some time constraints, such as a fixed examination date and a cohort of learners working at much the same time, you may need to have a time structure. You will need to decide whether each item of continuous assessment should be submitted by a fixed date and, if so, how far you are prepared to vary these dates for learners who fall behind with their work and may, consequently, be in danger of *drop-out*. Without a firm 'cut-off' date, of course, you can only give limited feedback to those learners who submit their work in good time; otherwise you run the risk of giving unfair help to those who have not yet sent in their work. It is also necessary to make it clear whether every learner has to submit every assignment, or whether there is also to be a clearly-defined amount of flexibility in this respect. A system for recording the marks and reporting them back to the learner is needed, along with a system for returning the teaching *feedback* on the assignment. It should be possible for learners to know their standing at any time, so that they are encouraged by ongoing success, or perhaps spurred to greater efforts by the possibility of not attaining their goal.

copyright In preparing self-instructional material, we often want to draw on the work of other people. Indeed we would expect to do so for, as teachers we expect to benefit from and pass on the experience and knowledge of others. We can, however, run into legal difficulties with the way we use other people's material if we breach copyright legislation. Writing parts of a book on the blackboard for people to copy down might be acceptable (or at least unobserved) but photocopying chunks of material for inclusion within your teaching and for distribution to learners may well infringe the law.

For education and training, some legal concessions are recognized, but not many. You should, therefore, be careful about copying or otherwise reproducing material belonging to someone else. This applies to print, films, illustrations, photographs, computer software, sound recordings and broadcast programmes. You may need to get copyright clearance, which can cost nothing or be rather expensive. Cartoons, for example, which are very popular among teachers attempting to relate academic studies to current everyday experience, can be very costly.

There are ways of using other people's work in your materials which involve the inclusion of the item, book, article, video or whatever in its entirety. It will then be accompanied by a *study guide* or *workbook* which you have written to guide the learners' interaction with that material. You might purchase and provide the material as part of the package or expect the learner to purchase the material to put with the package. (See also *wrap-around*.)

counselling in open and distance learning refers to educational counselling – that advice and encouragement that people need, in addition to subject-specific support, to help them be successful learners. It may be help with educational planning and course choice, the development of study skills, vocational guidance, steering through administrative systems or support in coping with the combination of part-time study, working and family life. Counselling may be the responsibility of course providers or tutors or may be provided by a specialist educational counsellor.

course guide is the component of a course which helps learners to find their way around the course material or package. It usually includes a description of the course, possibly with aims and objectives, who it is aimed at and how it relates to other courses or packages; a description of the course components, how to make use of them and advice about other things, such as a set book, resource material or equipment, to which the learner must have access; possible routes through the course; a study and assignment schedule, if appropriate; details of tutorial and other support arrangements; and any administrative information. (See also *study guide*.)

course presentation and monitoring Once the course material is ready, the twin tasks of presentation and monitoring begin. Course presentation includes the routine tasks necessary for the smooth running of the course. Monitoring is a more evaluative activity, involving the collection of feed-back with a view to further development of the course.

Much of the work of course presentation is administrative but the arrangements for any *tutorial support*, the marking of *assignments* and general responsibility for examinations are all integral parts of the teaching of the course; so is the devising of fresh test questions for *continuous assessment* and *examinations*. Marketing the course and recruiting students may also be part of course presentation.

Course monitoring is essential if there is to any form of *curriculum development*. Even if your draft materials have been subject to *developmental testing* they will not be perfect. Through course monitoring you will get to know how effective the materials are when they are being used in earnest by learners. If you yourself are involved with materials preparation, tutorial support, grading assignments and marking examinations, you will be in the best possible position to improve the materials in the light of experience. If other people carry out these tasks you will need to make arrangements for suitable *feedback* to be collected and made available to whoever is responsible for whatever changes, rewriting, etc. are necessary or possible. The job of developing high-quality learning materials is by no means over when you have produced a final draft for printing.

course teams Open and distance learning material can be prepared by individuals just as face-to-face courses are taught by individual teachers. However, when materials are being prepared on a large scale it is usual for a team of people to be responsible, somewhat akin to team teaching. A course team may comprise a variety of people with skills in and responsibilities for different aspects or stages of the production process: subject matter experts, educational technologists, television/audio producers, editors, illustrators/designers, and such like.

criterion-referenced assessment Whenever we assess a learner's performance (and for that matter whenever a learner uses *self-assessment*) there has to be some standard against which to arrive at a judgement. If we judge the learner against some standard we have fixed beforehand, we are using criterion-referenced assessment. (For a discussion of the alternative, see *norm-referenced assessment*.)

Many learners are hoping to achieve some formal proof of success – a certificate, a diploma, or a degree – and in that sense have chosen criterion-referenced assessment. They, as well as the teacher/assessor, need to know whether they are on course for final success. In a face-to-face situation learners get a good deal of both formal and informal *feedback* as to their progress. Distance learners usually get this sort of information from criterion-referenced *continuous assessment*. Learners' own self-assessment may also give useful information, although some of it may consist of questions that are intended to make it easy for them to learn, rather than for reliable criterion-referenced self-testing. Nonetheless, when distance learners check the answers to self-assessment questions, they are likely to jump to the conclusion that their performance is below standard if they do not get many of them right - they are likely to assume that there is an element of criterion-referenced assessment in such questions. Bear this in mind when you include such questions in your self-instructional material and, especially, when you discuss the answers.

curriculum development The curriculum is the total structure of ideas and educational experiences making up any one educational system or its component parts and curriculum development is the global term we apply to any systematic process intended to develop this structure. It includes:

- Decisions on the course structure as a whole;
- The formulation of *aims* and *objectives*;
- Decisions on the content to be included;
- The teaching strategy and methods to be used;
- *Media choice*;
- *Assessment* techniques;
- *Evaluation.*

Most of these, of course, are much the same kinds of decisions as those regularly made on a smaller scale by each individual teacher. If self-instructional materials are being developed on a large scale by teams of people, the management of curriculum development may be the responsibility of an educational technologist or an instructional designer. (See *educational technology*).

D

delivery in open and distance learning usually refers to the arrangements by which materials are made available to learners. Before you begin to plan and prepare materials you need to have a fairly clear idea of the delivery system you will be operating within and what constraints or opportunities this implies. Although in practice very few of us have anything like a free choice of delivery systems, we need to be aware of the ever-increasing alternatives which modern technology has to offer and have some idea of the hardware and organizational implications.

Our materials are still predominantly text-based and there are good reasons why this is likely to remain so in many fields (see *media choice*). Even with printed materials there are things to be organized if learners are going to get the right things at the right time. For example: are you going to have just-in-time printing or electronic delivery of text to remote distribution points or will you have to arrange storage for a large quantity of print materials? Will you need to take possible postal delays into account? Will the materials go to the learner or will the learner come to the materials? Are you going to centralize, or would it be more appropriate to route learners through local study centres or places of employment? What items of equipment, such as video-recorders or computers, will learners have access to and what might you have to provide for them? Answering some of these questions may call for more than just logistics; it may be good strategy to involve tutors, employers and groups of learners in the delivery process so they feel personally committed to, and hence willing to provide a measure of support for the project.

In times of constant and rapid improvement and change of potential delivery systems, it is hard to make rules for decision-taking. We can only be aware of all the possibilities, decide what is possible and appropriate in the particular set of circumstances, keep abreast of innovations, and try to make each decision a one-off event that does not constrain future options.

developmental testing, field trial or pilot is a kind of formative evaluation that usually consists of trying out materials, courses, teaching strategies, etc. on learners with a view to collecting *feedback* that can be used to improve the teaching. It is, of course, highly desirable to arrange for testing to be carried out as a routine procedure whenever the materials are in use and this sort of development is often associated with course monitoring (see *course presentation and monitoring*). Developmental testing is often conducted on draft materials with a small group of learners, carried out early enough to leave time for any necessary improvements to be made before the course proper is available to the main body of learners. However, if your learner numbers are small and your system flexible enough to make any necessary modifications as you go along, you may find course monitoring is enough to ensure satisfactory development of your materials.

Whether or not you are contemplating a field trial, a useful first stage of developmental testing is to give a draft of your materials to colleagues who can be relied upon to be objective without seeming hostile and who are familiar with the potential learner audience. Having discussed and incorporated their comments, a *tutorial try-out* with four or five learners can be very helpful. This cheap and relatively easily organized developmental process should be enough to accomplish the first, modest and most realistic aim of developmental testing, which is the elimination of any major errors or weaknesses from your materials – if you have included a wrong or inappropriate diagram or an exercise that cannot be done, you will soon find out.

If you have time, resources, potentially very large student numbers and subject matter that will be valid for a considerable length of time, you may consider organizing a field trial of the draft materials in order to make further improvements. This, typically, will involve you in assembling a representative sample of potential learners, pre-testing them, having them work through the materials in typical study conditions, post-testing them and collecting their detailed reactions by means of proformas, questionnaires and/or interviews. On a large enough scale such a process can yield results that can be expressed in a quantitative way and analysed statistically to reveal any subtle underlying patterns. The simple developmental gains may not however, justify the outlay. Before deciding on a field trial some hard questions need to be addressed.

- Where will you find a suitable learner sample? Quite apart from the technical difficulties of devising a statistically valid sample that will respond in full and on time, experience tends to show that you may find it difficult to get access to the correct target population. If, for example, you are developing third-year materials, the students on whom you would want to test them are usually too busy with their current second year work to try out your materials in a satisfactory way.

- How many different learning styles and study strategies will be represented in your sample and how far will these affect your results? If your sample is drawn from a relatively uniform total population (educationally speaking) you may be able to draw reasonably firm conclusions from your results; a great range of ability and a mixture of educational backgrounds among your learners, on the other hand, can present you not only with sampling problems but also with puzzling, or even contradictory results.
- Will the draft materials resemble the final product closely enough? Learners' reactions to drafts may not be an entirely safe guide to their reactions to the final, glossier, edited, well-illustrated product.
- Is it possible to test all the materials together and in the right order? It is relatively rare for all the components of a package to be ready for developmental testing at the same time, but to test components in isolation from each other is to invite spurious results because no account will be taken of the interactions (both intended and unintended) between the individual components of the package and the cumulative effects.
- Will the sample of learners be motivated to the same extent as the student body proper? If no certificate, no formal grade, no promotion, no official pass/fail result depends upon their performance, they are 'armchair critics' and can take risks and short cuts that genuine learners would not.
- Will you have enough time to collect the data, process them, interpret the results and identify the weaknesses? Like all the other processes in developing learning materials, this always takes longer than you think.
- Having established the weaknesses, will you have the resources to put them right? If the key person who first prepared the materials is no longer available, if the recording studio is fully booked, or if time presses in some other way, you may find yourself having to distribute the final product without making the modifications you know to be necessary.

Unless you have confident answers to questions like the above, you will not in practice be able to sustain the rigorous approach that is, in theory, the most attractive feature of field trials. All the resources allocated to a field trial may be a poor investment. You may find it quicker, as informative and certainly cost-effective, to compromise by staging something less ambitious and less rigidly controlled. For example, you might devise a set of open-ended questions to which any roughly suitable group of learners could respond. The information you would collect might be less 'hard', but as with a tutorial try-out, it would be up to you to use your own judgement and experience to interpret the results. It is always better to be sure of responding quickly to some immediate feedback than to collect a mass of expensive data which are insufficiently used.

diagnostic tests see *pre-tests, remedial material.*

diagrams are graphic visualizations of processes and relationships and are widely used in learning materials. It is helpful to contrast them with pictures since they use many of the same graphic techniques in quite different ways. While pictures *describe* the surface experience of things or places, diagrams *explain* how they work and how they relate to one another in abstract rather than spatial ways. Pictures therefore answer questions of 'what', 'where', and 'who'; diagrams answer questions of 'why', 'when' and 'what if'. In a picture, the use of colour, line and shading represents the artist's attempts to imitate a visual reality but the same things may be used purely symbolically in a diagram. A typical road map illustrates this point well, because it employs both conventions at once: using colour realistically – the sea being portrayed as blue and forests as green; using colour symbolically – motorways being shown in blue and ordinary roads in red. In a diagram, pictorial realism may often be used but only if it does not interfere with the main purpose of explanation. There are three main types of diagram:

1. Systems or network diagrams. Many diagrams show how the components of systems or networks of concepts relate to one another. A single diagram may use more than one graphic technique to show different kinds of relationship. The two major graphic techniques are: (a) The Venn convention, where shaded or boxed areas of space (representing categories of concepts) may be overlapped or separated according to the relationships to be portrayed, (see Figure 2). (b) The flow chart convention, where boxes representing concepts are linked by arrows or lines representing various kinds of connections (see Figure 3).

The relationships these techniques may display include hierarchical structures, flows and processes, domains of responsibility, or simple networks or connections. Some subject areas (chemistry, computing and electronics, for example) have special conventions for such diagrams, but they are also used in a general way in other areas.

2. Diagnostic charts and algorithms. Diagrams may also be used to aid decision-making. Diagnostic charts can show how a mechanical system works in such a way that it is possible to select appropriate tests to identify faults. Algorithms represent the alternative outcomes from various combinations of conditions: the reader is asked a series of questions and directed along different paths according to the response. (See Figure 4).

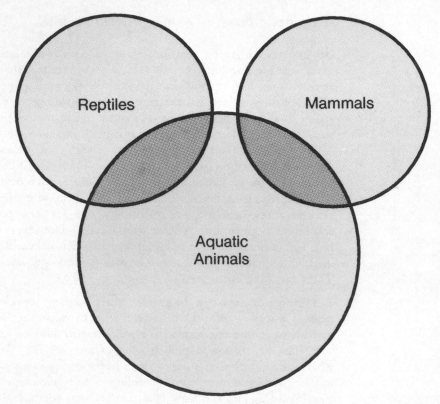

Figure 2 *A simple Venn diagram: some reptiles are aquatic animals and some mammals are aquatic animals; no reptiles are mammals*

3. Exploded diagrams and assembly charts. Diagrammatic and pictorial conventions may be combined to create illustrations that explain how a mechanism is assembled. (See Figure 5).

Under ***illustrations*** you will find lists of general purposes, guidelines and problems that also apply to diagrams. Here are four further points:

- Because they use special conventions in systematic ways, diagrams may be considered as a form of graphic language. It may be necessary to ensure that your learners are familiar with that language – perhaps by teaching them to interpret diagrams early on in the material or course.

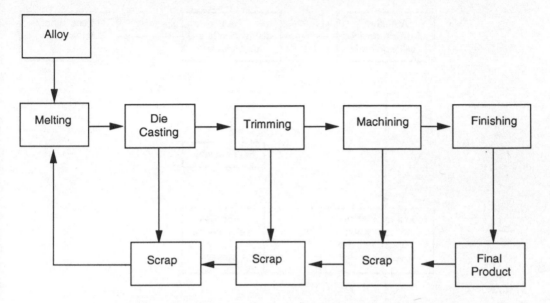

Figure 3 *A flow chart for the production of a die-cast component*

Diagrams will be wasted as a teaching/learning aid if they are not accessible to the learner.

A language is not only a means of communication, but also a tool for thinking with. Both you and your learners may use diagrams for organizing your ideas and planning your activities.

- Try to make the overall pattern of the diagram clear. If it is a tree-structure or a cyclical process, emphasize that fact.
- The pattern of a diagram should arise from the relationships being displayed, not from a formal pattern imposed on them for decorative reasons; there is no need to make a diagram symmetrical just to make it look neat. If there is symmetry it should show something significant, for example, that two parts of an organization are similarly structured.
- If a diagram becomes too complex, consider dividing it into several separate diagrams. Sometimes you can do this by using the same overall pattern in a series of diagrams each of which displays a different aspect of the subject, eg political, physical, climatic, geological and agricultural maps of the same country.

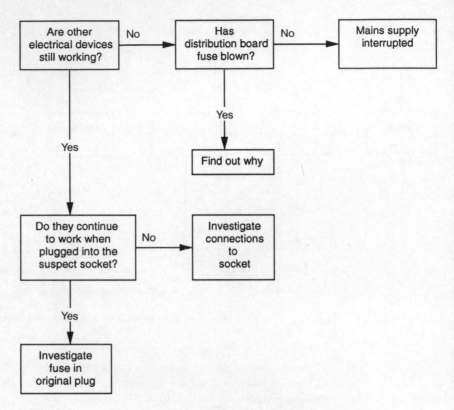

Figure 4 *A simple algorithm for tracing an electrical fault*

disabled see *people with disabilities.*

discussion see *self-help groups, tutorial support.*

distance (and open) learning/learners A key question for any-one preparing materials or designing a system for open or distance learning is, 'What do we mean by open and distance learners and how do they differ from other learners?'.

All learners who use self-instructional materials whether in open, distance or flexible systems are, to some extent, distance learners. The use of self-instructional materials implies that learners are studying at one remove from the author who, by preparing the learning materials, is effectively their principal

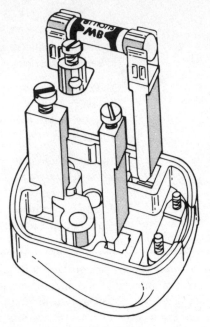

Figure 5   *Exploded diagram of an electrical plug*

What do we mean by open and distance learners/learning?

Characteristics of distance students	*Implications for the design of learning materials*
Low level of support	Reduce uncertainty to the minimum. Make clear and full explanations. Address the student as 'you', using an informal, friendly *style*.
Lack of any immediate feedback	Include an adequate amount of *self-assessment*. Turn around assignments quickly, with *feedback*.
Lack of study time	Lay down strict rules for any claims made on it.

continued

Characteristics of distance students	Implications for the design of learning materials
	Make realistic time estimates for every component. Be prepared to trim the total if necessary.
Short intermittent study periods	Include an adequate supply of *access devices*. Sum up at the end of each stage. Briefly recapitulate at the beginning of each stage.

teacher. Even in those systems where face-to-face tutorial support is provided there is rarely any guarantee that the support tutor is permanently available. Indeed the fact that learners can pursue their studies in their own way, in their own time and in places of their choosing is probably the biggest single advantage of, and motive for, providing self-instructional materials. All learners who use materials of this kind, then, are either actual or potential distance learners.

Think of the rich and complex support system that is available to an in-college or on-site learner. Then ask yourself how much of this support is available to learners working on their own, using self-instructional materials at their own chosen time and place. The short answer is little or none and the learning materials must compensate for this lack of support. Distance learners are invariably part-time students with work and family commitments so the time they can devote to study is limited and long periods of intensive study may be few and far between. These learners may be people returning to formal study, with little preparation or very rusty study experience. There are, therefore likely to be considerable differences between these learners and full-time college-based students and these differences have implications of the utmost importance for the design of self-instructional materials.

distribution of materials see *delivery*.

drop-out is the term for learners ceasing to be active in their course of study before its completion and is a concern in any form of education or training. There are additional factors which may exacerbate it in open and distance learning. These learners are often highly-motivated and eager to learn but they are also faced with special problems. They are frequently part-time students and so have to contend with the demands of family and work. They often get less support from tutors and fellow-learners. They may also be inadequately prepared to start studying at a distance. No matter how well the materials and the systems are designed, some learners will drop out. There are some measures you can take to minimize drop-out.

- Make sure that prospective learners get an accurate description of what they are to study and what it will entail. For instance, if it is a course, they should know its content, *objectives*, level, approach, *prerequisites* and *workload*.
- Courses tend to have lower drop-out rates if learners are 'paced', ie, if their pace of study is regulated. Fixed starting and completion dates, for assignments and other activities, can help learners along provided there is some flexibility so that learners are not forced to drop out if circumstances prevent them from sending in one assignment.
- Most drop-out occurs very early in the course, at or before the first of the *assignments*. Making this assignment relatively easy or purely formative may help overcome this psychological barrier.
- Learners need to know quickly how well they are doing. Swift *feedback* on assignments is essential.
- Learners should be able to telephone or otherwise get in touch with tutors or counsellors who can help them with any problem associated with their studies.
- Learners can be put in touch with others taking the same course to form a *self-help group*.
- You may be able to modify the later stages of the course as a result of information gathered on the problems experienced by learners early in the course. (See *course presentation and monitoring*.)

Monitoring the learners to establish how many are dropping out and at what stages gives valuable information. You may be able to find out which types of learners are likely to drop out and do something to help them particularly. On the other hand, drop-out is not easy to detect until long after the event in many cases. When does a learner who is badly behind become a drop-out? Do you have a mechanism which encourages people to inform you?

When deciding what to change in your materials, you will be in a better position to make improvements if you can draw on reasons given for dropping out and on the reactions of successful learners. Those who have tutored the course will also be able to suggest changes.

But don't be too gloomy about drop-out! Even the best courses with the best materials have their drop-outs. Job changes, illness, marriage and many other life circumstances will always claim a certain percentage of your learners. Bear in mind too that dropping-out is not always a negative experience for the learner. Some start off never intending to complete the course, some abandon it when it has met their immediate needs, and others will be so encouraged by what they learn from you that they transfer in mid-stream to an even more demanding course.

E

editing As far as self-instructional materials are concerned, editing is the process by which draft materials are made ready for reproduction and distribution. It is very much concerned with *quality control*. The editor is normally responsible for the textual accuracy and, to some extent, the appearance of the final product; if he or she is an academic editor, there will also be the ultimate responsibility for the academic standard of what has been written. An editor's contributions usually include most of the following:

- Ensuring that the draft is of a suitable length, that it conforms to the brief that the author has been given (if any), and is at a level of intelligibility appropriate to the readership.
- Checking on spelling, punctuation, paragraphing, headings, proper names, etc, paying special attention to consistency and conforming to any rules for 'house style'.
- Fitting into place any components not in the original draft, such as *glossaries*, *illustrations* and *indexes*. Seeing that captions are correctly matched to illustrations and preparing contents lists, the title page, etc.
- Listing footnotes and seeing that cross-referencing is correct and consistent.
- Preparing the final draft for the form of printing process that is being used.
- Reading proofs, if necessary.
- Keeping the whole process on schedule.
- Making tactful suggestions as to improvements.
- If the materials are being prepared by more than one person, identifying and flagging useful cross-linkings where the same topic crops up in different pieces of material – links of which the authors themselves may be unaware.
- Similarly, identifying places where different authors are giving inconsistent, or even contradictory, accounts of the same thing.
- Going over all proposed alterations with the author, who must always have the last word.

If you are preparing your own materials for your own learners you may well have to be your own editor. If you are taking part in a collaborative project, as a member of a *course team*, for example, you may find yourself having to edit other peoples' work. This responsibility may form part of a planned strategy, which has been decided by the course team.

Alternatively, you may, unfortunately, find yourself pressed into service because someone else's inadequacies have led to an emergency situation. Whether or not the material you are editing is your own, you should be aware that editors are important setters and maintainers of standards of excellence and, above all, that to edit anything properly takes time. From the very start of the process of preparing your materials you should allow ample time for editing.

educational technology is a rather diverse field but basically it is the study, and application, of techniques, systems, tools and media used in education and training. Through a systems approach, educational technology attempts to maximize the efficiency of methods by which knowledge and skills can be passed on. In the preparation of learning materials, an educational technologist will analyse the needs of the learners and organize the most effective means of delivering learning to satisfy those needs. This process will include determining who the learners are likely to be, what is to be learned, where the learning will take place, what equipment and *tutorial support* will be available, possibly developing a new teaching technique for a particular application, putting material through *developmental testing*, designing an *assessment* system and evaluating the outcome of the materials. (See also *curriculum development*.)

end-test see *post-test*.

enrichment material is material that extends and/or further illustrates a topic that has already been studied. If your estimates of workload are reasonably accurate, an average learner will have just about enough time to master the normal lesson material that is offered. There will always be some, however, who are faster, more enthusiastic, or for some reason have more time than their fellows. Enrichment material is potentially of interest to all learners, but in practice is usually intended for this latter group.

The exact nature of provision for enrichment depends, to some extent, on the time and other resources at your disposal:

- Minimum provision – referring the learner to other resources, eg, a reading list (assuming that library resources are available), or other suitable in-house material.
- Moderate provision – including activities and exercises of increasing difficulty as optional extras.

- Major provision – preparing extra learning material to examine more closely, or to extend, some of the points dealt with in the main material.

entry behaviour see *prerequisites.*

entry tests see *pre-tests.*

evaluation is the process by which we arrive at a judgement as to the educational effectiveness of anything, from a lesson to a course or a whole curriculum. (In the USA the word 'evaluation' is also applied to students and the process of measuring learner attainment – what in the UK is called *assessment*). Several important things to be asked whenever you are planning any form of evaluation are:

- What criteria of success are you going to use?
- What data are you going to collect and in what way?
- How are you going to process them?
- Who, apart from yourself, wants the information?
- What, if anything, are you going to do as a result of the evaluation?

You will need to decide, therefore, what you are looking for, how you are going to look for it, how you will know whether you've found it or not, how you will report your findings and to whom. You will then have to think about courses of action in the light of these findings.

There are two main approaches for you to choose from, or to combine in some way:

'Agro-botany' type evaluation is based upon a scientific model which has been compared to agricultural research. It usually decides in advance what criteria of success it is going to use. It emphasizes aspects that can be expressed in numbers, and is therefore likely to concern itself with such things as enrolment, *drop-out, assessment*, etc, which can easily be quantified. It often uses survey research methods in general, and questionnaires in particular, in order to quantify attitudes and opinions.

'Illuminative evaluation' emphasizes the more qualitative aspects of evaluation and has more in common with ethnography and social anthropology. It is less likely to take any predetermined stance and tries to be flexible enough to modify its strategy in the light of experience gained during the actual investigation. It uses observation, interviews, discussion, informal conversations, etc., to establish what the people most concerned think and feel about the course, curriculum, or institution being evaluated.

There is much debate about the relative merits of these two approaches when applied to relatively large-scale evaluations conducted by outside, independent evaluators. Most teachers and trainers, however, operate on a much smaller scale, are insiders, and are less concerned with the whole curriculum and the whole institution than with their own contribution to it. When you evaluate your own course and your own materials at a commonsense level (and it is important to do so at regular intervals if they are to improve or remain successful and relevant to a changing audience) it would be surprising if you took no notice of such quantifiable things as the number of learners registering, the drop-out rate, the distribution of assessment grades, or examination results. It would be equally surprising if you did not also take into account such qualitative things as your colleagues' opinions and feelings as well as your learners' opinions and feelings. You would almost certainly draw on both the approaches described above. (See also *course presentation and monitoring*, *developmental testing*, *feedback* and *tutorial try-out*.)

examinations are one rather formal means by which a person's learning may be assessed. Most examinations are more *summative* than *formative* and take place at the end of courses that they are intended to assess. They usually include arrangements for:

- Invigilators exercising strict control.
- A specified and enclosed venue, the 'examination room'.
- A time limit that is strictly adhered to.
- The prohibition of any form of help to candidates other than the use of specified reference books or calculators.
- A question paper that candidates see for the first time when the examination begins.
- All candidates tackling the same questions, or having the same choice of questions.
- No immediate second chance, in some cases no second chance at all, for those who fail.

Examinations of this type are not always an appropriate means of assessing certain types of courses or certain categories of learner but there are quite strong reasons for these strict conditions, especially reasons to do with academic acceptability and validity of accreditation.

Examinations can be stressful for anyone but open and distance learners are likely to feel the stress particularly acutely since one great advantage they enjoy is to be free to pursue their studies in their own way with a minimum of control – the antithesis of the examination room. It is unfortunate for them that final examinations are often considered to be an important, indeed indispensable, feature of assessment, particularly in a distance education system.

There are two main reasons for this:

- Although learners may have submitted several *assignments* as part of their *continuous assessment*, the examination may be the first time that they come into personal contact with the institution. Where the award of a certificate or some other form of qualification is at stake, and they are not known personally to their teachers, it is necessary for learners to appear in person and identify themselves.
- Since their assignments have, presumably, been completed with the help of some or all of the resources at their disposal – materials, books, notes, friends, relations, etc – it may be felt necessary to test the knowledge, skills and personal qualities that they can deploy unaided.

If you feel that too much examination stress is counterproductive for your learners but you cannot eliminate examinations altogether, the stress can be reduced in various ways:

- Notifying the questions some time – 14 days, say – before the examination so that the learners come to the examination room well-prepared. The standard expected (and the standard of work usually produced) is naturally higher. The possibility of the regurgitation of someone else's efforts also becomes higher.
- Allowing the learners a certain amount of specified reference material, so that the examination situation becomes more like a real-life project, which depends partly on their familiarity with, and skill in selecting and using, their resources.
- At the very least, familiarizing learners with the layout of the examination paper by providing a specimen paper exactly comparable in all but the detail of the questions with the actual one. Perhaps a piece of continuous assessment can be presented as a practice examination paper, so that learners can practise examination techniques and have their efforts commented on before the examination takes place.

external contributors You may want to employ other people to help you to prepare your self-instructional materials, perhaps to help with course design, writing or evaluation. In this way you can get expert help with content or technique, or maybe secure someone prestigious who will put a seal of approval on your work and even help you to publicize the materials. Or you may want to collaborate with colleagues from another institution who want materials to teach a similar course and with whom you can share the workload.

Useful external contributors are those who have experience in open or distance learning, those who want to learn about it, those who want to help you or your institution, and of course people who have additional subject-matter expertise that you need for your course. Avoid those who seem unable to adapt to your needs, who just want to get their own ideas published, or who are so busy that their promised contribution will be the first thing to go if time presses them too hard. Using the same external contributors for different tasks makes sense, as they will need less briefing each time.

Unless you are able to operate in a fairly informal way, a well-written contract may prevent problems. Try to include a detailed description of the task, including the aims and objectives of the piece of self-instructional material to be written, or what reports to write, which meetings or discussions to attend, how many drafts of materials to produce, whether to include activities, test questions, and so on. You should include the scheduling arrangements of what you need and when. Some contracts have penalties for late delivery. External contributors should know the position on *copyright* and on attribution of their work, and whether their work is going to be edited, adapted or used without their prior agreement. It helps to cut up the task into stages, so that you can end an unsatisfactory contributor's contract before too much harm is done. Also bear in mind that, as the project progresses, you may want to change it, sometimes quite radically, and that the external contribution as originally contracted may no longer be appropriate, however good it is.

External contributors do get confused by changes of plan – they are rarely privy to all the discussions about a course or materials – and sometimes find they are in touch with too many people. If you are working as a team, designate somebody as contact person. Regardless of what is in the contract, some contributors resent suggestions for change and editing. Some find it easier to accept when they know that in open and distance teaching everyone's drafts get amended.

You can help your external contributors by briefing them well on why you need their contribution, for which learners it is intended, how it fits into the rest of the course, and how it will be used. If you need a simple introduction to the subject for your learners, and you end up with a piece of high technology or lofty erudition elaborating on the latest research, it will be the contributor's fault only if *you* stated the job clearly in the first place.

F

face-to-face components of open and distance learning are those occasions on which a learner, or group of learners, comes together with a teacher or tutor for a planned learning experience. This may be a tutorial, a residential school or a counselling or guidance session. The phrase 'face-to-face' is sometimes used to denote conventional, on-site teaching or training in contrast to distance education.

feedback is a useful concept, borrowed from cybernetics, meaning the way in which information about what is happening in one part of a system is fed back to another part where, if necessary, corrective action can be taken. Of great importance in education and training, feedback can often be translated as 'knowledge of results'. When we are learning, we need to know how far we are getting things right, and in what ways we need to improve. We ourselves are not usually the best judge of this, but we need to get feedback from somewhere, for without it there is unlikely to be any development.

In face-to-face teaching there should be plenty of feedback available to the learner, both formal and informal. It may take the form of test scores or written or spoken comments on *assignments* that have been submitted. It may come from learners comparing work with one another, or hearing their comments on one another's efforts. Feedback is equally necessary for open and distance learners but much of what has been mentioned will not normally be available to them. Feedback needs to be built into self-instructional materials in terms of the answers to and discussion of *questions*, *activities* and *self-assessment* exercises. This might even include suggestions of where to go back to or a different approach to take to the material. Another important source of feedback for distance learners is a tutor's marks and comments on their assignments and for maximum educational effectiveness such assignments should always be returned to learners as soon as possible.

But feedback to learners is only half the picture. Teachers and managers need feedback as well. You need feedback on the progress of each group of learners, and detailed feedback on the progress of each individual learner. Much of this will come in the form of *assessment* results and you can use these to start to make judgements about the effectiveness of your learning materials. You will need feedback on other things as well because test scores do not give a complete picture. Satisfactory test scores may only be achieved because learners are spending double or treble the amount of time that has been suggested for the materials. Later on this could lead to high *drop-out* and other problems. Again, satisfactory test scores overall may mask the fact that certain parts of the materials are relatively ineffective and place unnecessary obstacles in the learners' way. And what if many of them are late in submitting their assignments? Is there some reason for this? If you have little or no opportunity to talk to your learners, how will you get to know?

In open and distance education we sometimes need to make special arrangements to gather in feedback that would be automatically available if we were continually interacting with them. You can do this in three main ways:

- Take every opportunity to visit, and talk to, your learners.
- Talk to, or get written information from, any teachers who are in contact with your learners, eg, those who are providing the element of tutorial support.
- Collect written information direct from learners.

To collect written comments, you might want to use questionnaires of some kind. One useful and relatively easy way of doing this is to take advantage of the fact that assessment results may well be the one form of regular feedback we can count on receiving. When learners complete assignments, you can ask them also to complete a number of short questions about the assignment and, more importantly, their reactions to the learning materials on which the assignment was based. These comments can then be submitted along with the assignment. If there are tutors other than you who who mark and comment on learners' assignments, you can ask them to submit not only a list of gradings, but also a report upon such things as the general level of performance and common errors that have cropped up in a number of assignments. The responses from learners and tutors which you collect in this way will ensure that you have a regular flow of feedback which will tell you what things need to be changed, although not necessarily how to do it. (See *course presentation and monitoring*.)

There are other occasions when you deliberately set out to gather feedback. Any formal *evaluation* process, for example, is a deliberate attempt to collect feedback with a view to making a judgement as to how well the course and/or the materials and/or the institution are working. *Developmental testing*, *tutorial try-outs* and field trials of self-instructional materials are deliberate attempts to collect significant feedback from which you can make the decisions on which all development depends. But there is no point in organizing the collection of feedback if you do not intend to do anything about it. Feedback by itself can never be anything more than interesting; it is what you do with it that counts.

field trial see *developmental testing*.

flexible learning is a term used to describe many learning systems which could just as well be called 'open'. The word 'flexible' tends to emphasize the individualized nature of the programme; that it is designed to offer the maximum opportunity to every possible learner. A definition offered by the National Council for Educational Technology is:

> . . . a means of making it possible for learners to gain access to education and training provision tailored to their needs and aspirations.

The term is sometimes favoured because people believe it makes more obvious what is implied than does 'open learning'. Flexible learning is no more tightly defined than is open learning and the terms are often used synonymously.

fog index see *readability*.

format see *presentation*.

formative evaluation is the process of collecting and analysing information about institutions, courses, materials and so on so that they may be improved. If evaluation were being used merely to arrive at a judgement as to the success (or otherwise) of the course, etc, it would be *summative* evaluation. *Developmental testing* is a good example of formative evaluation, because it is intended as part of the ongoing process of improving the materials, and not to provide any overall judgement on them.

The same two phrases can be applied to the evaluation of learner performance, ie formative or summative *assessment*. The tutor's comments on any assignment or exercise that is not graded are an example of purely formative assessment. A final *examination*, by contrast, is an example of summative assessment which is carried out principally so that judgements can be made, recorded and published. It cannot have much formative value for learners, since it usually comes too late for them to modify their studies in any way.

It is interesting to note, however, that examinations can also act as formative evaluation for you, as the teacher, if you analyse the results in order to discover your learners' common errors, in the hope that you can improve the learning materials for the next users.

Most types of formal assessment, in fact, have both summative and formative aspects, since they usually result in grades being recorded, as well as providing information on which teachers and/or learners can improve their teaching and learning. One kind of assessment that is purely formative is *self-assessment*, because its purpose is always to improve the learning process and never, even as a by-product to arrive at an official mark or grading.

frame is an individual portion of the learning material. In audiovision it is the page of text, illustration, table or whatever being studied at that time and is often boxed or framed and numbered for ease of identification. In computer-based learning, it is a screenful of information which may be reproduced as hard copy.

G

glossaries are lists in alphabetical order of key terms, usually followed by their definitions. They are useful in subject areas that have their own distinctive terminology or that employ commonly used words in a special way. Glossaries can take various forms. One may consist of a list of terms only, with a cross-reference to the place in the materials where each term is introduced and defined; this type functions more like a limited *index*. Alternatively, a separate booklet may be prepared with a list of terms and their definitions, together with a cross-reference to the place(s) in the materials where the terms are explained at greater length. Glossaries such as these are usually prepared for the whole of the materials covering complete courses, where they provide invaluable *access devices*. You will not normally need them for single lessons or a single component of a course.

Putting together a glossary can be an arduous undertaking and can not be done until near the end of the materials-preparation period. If you want to include page number references, etc, in order to help your learners, you may not be able to complete the glossary until page proofs have been prepared. But learners are grateful for glossaries and make good use of them particularly for *revision* and reviewing. The preparation of a glossary covering a whole course can also be useful in helping writers to avoid the unnecessary use of jargon and to be alert to inconsistencies in the use of technical terms, especially if the material is being prepared by a group of writers.

goals see *aims* and *objectives*.

graphs and charts see *diagrams* and *illustrations*.

H

headings are identifying labels that precede subdivisions of the text. They are used primarily as *access devices* and are worth considering carefully as you prepare self-instructional materials. Well designed they can help learners considerably; badly designed they can cause confusion. The effect, and consequently the wording of headings, depends to some degree on their position.

Cross-headings are placed within the column of text and are the most common type. Their effect is to label the passage that follows – by implication, the whole of the following text up to the next heading (of the same level, if there is a hierarchy). In practice the wording of cross-headings is determined by several competing considerations:

- They can act as a link between two parts of the text. The meaning of headings used in this way (which often include pronouns referring to ideas in the preceding text rather than a preceding heading, eg 'How it is used') is sometimes only clear to the careful reader rather than one who is using the headings as access devices. This access function is often better achieved within the text itself.
- They can identify a theme or a term that is then to be defined by the following text. Such headings may be useful to clarify the structure of the subject matter and for *revision* purposes, but relatively meaningless to the learner who is using the headings to preview the text. The addition of subheadings in ordinary language will satisfy both purposes, eg 'Autodidacticism – teaching yourself'.
- They can work together to summarize the structure of the text as a whole. Here, the wording of the heading must make sense not only in relation to the text immediately preceding or following it, but also in relation to all the other headings. When collected together as a contents list, therefore, they should present a coherent summary of the text in a way comprehensible to one who has not yet read it. Headings may be structured hierarchically for this purpose, using different type (eg smaller sizes) to signify their level. (See *presentation*.)

Side headings are placed in the margin. They can share the same functions as cross-headings but, because they do not interrupt the column of text (and therefore the flow of its argument), they can also provide a 'running commentary' on the argument, to be used as a *summary* or *overview*.

Running headings appear at the top (and sometimes at the foot) of the page. Some identify the title and the author of the text, and so have no special educational purpose. Those identifying the chapter title are rather more useful for access. Others identify the theme of the particular page and act in the same way as side headings.

icons are visual symbols which are often used to represent a range of actions or circumstances in open and distance learning materials (see Figure 6). They act as mental signposts and each icon is intended to signal the need for a particular action or response from the learner. If icons are carefully thought out, simple and clear, they are valuable as a form of visual shorthand. They remove the need for repeated written instructions and can signal, at a glance, the necessity for having to hand your audio-cassette player or that you will be expected to write something before the end of this particular section.

illustrations This term can describe the full range of graphic devices found in text, although its use is sometimes limited to pictures. There are four main approaches to illustration:

- **Pictures.** More or less realistic visual descriptions of real or imaginary places, people or objects. Pictures are not simple representations of reality, since they usually present just one of many possible aspects of the sub-

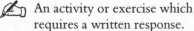
An activity or exercise which requires a written response.　　Discuss this with your tutor.

An assignment to be sent for marking.　　Feedback on questions and exercises.

An 'activity symbol'. Whenever you see this it means 'get going'. Learning should be active – not just reading what's provided, but seeking out answers and practising things for yourself.

Figure 6 *Examples of icons, or symbols, used in self-instructional material to alert learners to what is coming next*

ject. Even photographs are far from objective since the photographer can select the angle and the framing and focusing of the image, and can heavily influence such things as the contrast and brightness of the print. Drawings, of course, are often presented in a highly personal way by the artist in order to bring out particular points.

- **Diagrams.** Visualizations of processes and relationships (see *diagrams*). These may be of physical systems, such as mechanical or biological ones, or abstract systems, such as organizations or theories. A diagram of a physical system (an industrial process, for instance) may be shaped by the system itself, or it may use some other pattern in order to display a particular argument. For example, a flow chart of an industrial process can give learners a clear representation of separate sub-systems, together with their relationship to the system as a whole, although it would be quite impossible to distinguish these in the plant they would see on site.
- **Graphs, charts and quantitative displays**. These may be used to store data for easy retrieval, to display overall trends and other arguments about the data, or to discover new information from new combinations and representations of data. The usefulness to learners of any statistical graph or display depends upon the accuracy and accessibility of the detailed information it presents.
- **Maps and scale plans**. These are relatively small diagrams of the spatial layout of a large geographic area or man-made structure. Much of the information is to scale, eg, the linear dimensions of an architectural plan or the areas of countries and the distance between towns on a map. Some of it is not to scale, eg the width of a carriageway on a roadmap. Maps use a combination of pictorial techniques and coded symbols to show the spatial patterns of anything from capital cities and national frontiers to epidemic diseases or local dialects. By the ingenious use of symbols, colour and shading it is possible to squeeze a great deal of information into a single map.

Illustrations often fall into more than one of these four categories. TV weather maps, for example, are all four, being partly pictures, partly diagrams of meteorological processes, partly visual displays of quantitative information (temperature, pressure, wind direction and speed), and partly maps of a particular part of the world.

Illustrations can be an essential and integral part of the subject matter and stand on their own, or they can play a supportive role to the words in the text. They serve the following purposes:

- *description* – to show what something looks like when words are not enough in themselves, eg, the rings of Saturn;

- *explanation* – to show how a complex system works and how its parts interrelate, eg, a cutaway drawing;
- *demonstration* – to demonstrate a particular task to be carried out, eg, the way to measure a car engine's tappet clearances;
- *expression* – to elicit an emotional response in the learners, eg, humour, horror, sorrow, etc;
- *motivation* – to 'lighten' and add variety to a dense and/or long text, eg, contemporary political cartoons in a text on Victorian industrial legislation;
- *memorization* – to make an abstract concept more memorable by associating it with visual imagery, eg, an aerial photograph illustrating a mathematical treatment of location analysis.

Here are some guidelines which you may find useful when you are considering the use of illustrations:

- Always link the illustration explicitly with the text. Research shows that illustrations that are not directly referred to in the text are usually ignored by readers.
- Provide a full caption that discusses the illustration in detail and guides the learner's interpretation.
- Make learners examine the illustration carefully by accompanying it with questions or basing other *activities* on it.
- Print references in the text (eg, **See Figure 4**) in bold type or use other emphasis devices to make it easy to move from the illustration to the relevant part of the text.
- Place the illustration as near as possible to the major discussion of it in the text. If it is discussed again later, repeat it if you can (perhaps in miniature) or give learners the page reference.
- Never use an illustration that has no clear purpose. It will simply devalue the power of the medium and so diminish the impact of other purposeful illustrations.
- Always seek *copyright* permission before you reproduce other people's illustrations, including cartoons and comic strips. There is no graphic equivalent to the 'fair dealing' convention allowing you to quote short passages of text.

Illustrations are a form of communication with which your learners may not be familiar. Do not assume that they can read and interpret illustrations without some guidance. There are three main groups of problems connected with the use of illustrations:

- *Perceptual problems*. Various visual illusions can inadvertently confuse the learner's perception. An example is the figure/ground confusion shown in Figure 7.

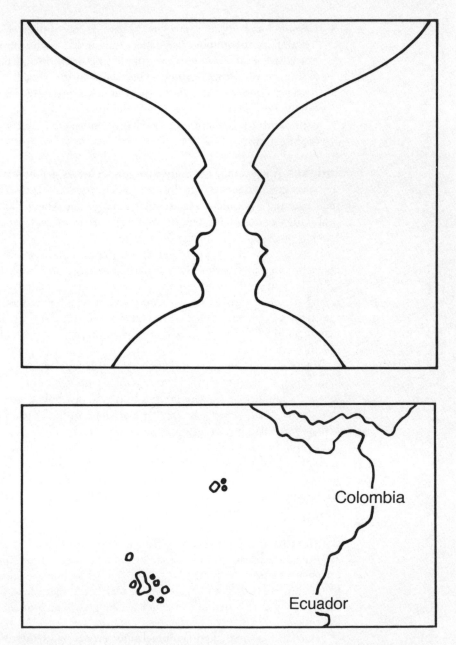

Figure 7 *Examples of figure/ground confusion: (a) the face/goblet confusion; (b) confusion between land and ocean on a map*

- *Cognitive and linguistic problems*. There is no universal 'grammar' or 'vocabulary' of graphic language – unfamiliar conventions or symbols can create a language barrier. Simple line drawing and perspective, for example, are not understood everywhere in the world.
- *Rhetorical problems*. The status of arguments presented in graphic form cannot be stated with the same subtlety as in text. There is no visual equivalent to 'sometimes', 'perhaps', 'normally' and other common qualifications.

indexes A good index is more than just an *access device* – it is an essential tool that enables learners to locate quickly particular subjects or items in their materials. An index is particularly important where the learner has to deal with a considerable number (40 pages or more, say) of rather similar-looking pieces of self-instructional material.

There are two main types of index, the general and the specific. The specific index is concerned with only one particular facet of a book or course. For example, you could have a specific index of all the names of people mentioned in the materials, or a specific index of all the Acts of Parliament referred to. A general index covers all the relevant items or 'keywords' and may include all the references that might otherwise appear in one or more specific indexes.

Where should the index go? If there is only one block of material to be considered, it should be placed at the end, as in most books. If the index has to cover a number of separate pieces of material (a whole course, for example) then the most useful index is one that is separate from the rest of the material, perhaps in a small booklet that can be used with any of the other components.

Compiling an index is a specialized task and you may need the services of an experienced indexer. Electronic and desktop publishing facilities usually include indexing but electronic choice of keywords and references can be too comprehensive and does not always give the emphasis you would have chosen. Some pruning may be necessary.

induction is the process by which learners are helped to understand the requirements, learning skills, mode of operation, etc, of an open or distance learning scheme. The induction component of a course is most likely to be text/audio-based or computer-based if that is the main medium. It may be available separately or built into the teaching structure of the early part of the course.

Induction is also an important process for producers, deliverers and supporters of open and distance learning materials. People new to open and distance learning will need to consider how this will differ from the teaching and training they have previously been involved with and assess what new skills they need to acquire.

information technology in the context of open and distance learning is technology for preparing, storing and presenting learning material, and technology for interpersonal communication particularly via computer. These include hard disks, CD-ROMs, laservision disks for storing materials, authoring tools and desktop publishing systems for preparing materials and any technology with visual and/or audible output, preferably with an inter-active capability, for the presentation of materials. (See also *computer-mediated communication*.)

instructional design see *curriculum development, educational technology.*

interactive television is a distance teaching tool being developed par-ticularly in rural North America. Learners and a tutor gather in small groups in several, widely geographically separated, TV studios for interactive seminar-style teaching. The studios are basic with just one camera and one technician and transmission is over dedicated telephone lines. Transmission can concentrate on the main contributer but monitor displays from each camera mean the tutor in particular can see each learner's reactions to the process. Visual material, including written text, can be shown to the camera and shared.

Course material and *assignments* are distributed in advance by post but fax machines can be used as back-up. Learners' assignments or other papers of immediate relevance can be distributed around the groups in a matter of minutes.

Similar ideas are being developed for interactive live-links via satellite. (See also *computer conferencing, teleconferencing, telephone tutorials*.)

interactive video is the interactive use of a combination of computer and video (tape or disc) for learning purposes. The combination is powerful enough to offer learners a great variety of learning strategies, even more than *computer-assisted learning*. The interactivity is pre-programmed by the designers but usually in a tutorial mode and learners can choose their own paths through the materials. Preparing interactive-video teaching is expensive and time-consuming because of the programming elements and the need for a great deal of suitable visual material and production costs are high. Conse-quently it can usually only be justified by economies of scale (where very large numbers will be taught), or if no other form of instruction can perform the same teaching task – or perhaps if someone else has already developed just the programme you need.

in-text questions (ITQs) are questions and activities that are to some extent embedded in the exposition or argument that is the main theme of the text itself. They are highly characteristic of self-instructional materials, corresponding, as they do, to the quick questions and activities that play such an important part in good face-to-face teaching. ITQs are often presented to learners in a distinctive pattern that makes it quite clear that they are being asked to do something before reading on.

Q. If you have not met in-text questions before, pause and think for a moment. What might an in-text question look like?

****

A. Like this!

Although there are many kinds of in-text question and *activities*, you have just attempted one very common kind of 'stop and think' question. The row of asterisks is one form of *student-stopper*, signalling the learners that you would like them to try to answer the question themselves before reading the answer you provide, and (providing they agree) preventing them from unintentionally reading the answer before they have had a chance to attempt the question. Some other examples of ITQs are given in Figure 8.

Most in-text questions fulfil more than one of a variety of functions:

- *Vigilance*. At the very least, having an occasional direct question aimed at them may stop learners sliding into passivity.
- *Self-assessment*. In-text questions together with all the other self-assessed testing devices can help learners to monitor their own progress.
- *Reinforcement*. People usually enjoy answering questions successfully and some psychologists suggest that this acts as a reward, helping to reinforce any learning that has taken place.
- *Highlighting*. It is perfectly possible to scatter in-text questions rather like currants in a cake. While this is better than having none at all, it is better still to use them to emphasize selected points in the text where there is a perceptible step forward in the teaching argument or exposition.
- *Linking*. If instead of marking the place where the teacher has taken a step forward, the learners, having been suitably prepared, are asked in an in-text question to take the next step forward themselves, the learning process can become a very active one, with all the advantages that are normally associated with active learning.

activity
7

Check the type and size of your school

Read the list below and tick your type of school.

- County?
- Voluntary aided?
- Voluntary controlled?
- Special agreement?
- Special school?

If you're not sure, look at the documents that you have been given by the LEA and the school or ask the Headteacher, Clerk or one of the other governors.

SAQ 5
Can you identify in this summary of Beale's thought another religious belief which guides his conclusions?

————————◄————————

The belief that God has created living things *purposefully*—that is, that He has designed things for the good of His creatures. One piece of living matter develops into a dog; another piece into a man. And the intricacy of structures like the brain's implies, for Beale, a divine designer and obvious purpose. Beliefs of this type—that processes are directed towards a goal—are called 'teleological'.

ITQ 3   Estimate where this continuum occurs by inspection of Figure 22. Check that this is in reasonable agreement with your extrapolation in Figure 23.

Enter here your estimate of the frequency at which the continuum starts.

Frequency, $f =$

Energy, $hf =$

Uncertainty limits $\pm$

What is the difference between his kind of living by rule-of-thumb and that represented by Vronsky, Anna and Oblonsky?

🙂🙂🙂🙂🙂🙂🙂🙂🙂🙂🙂🙂🙂🙂🙂🙂🙂🙂🙂🙂🙂🙂🙂🙂🙂🙂🙂🙂

10.25   **Discussion**

I would like to leave you to ponder this question, which is to some extent left open by Tolstoy, as other questions are, deliberately, left open by this epilogue. Indeed, you might like to ponder the reason for that fact (i.e. the fact that he leaves them open) also.

🙂🙂🙂🙂🙂🙂🙂🙂🙂🙂🙂🙂🙂🙂🙂🙂🙂🙂🙂🙂🙂🙂🙂🙂🙂🙂🙂🙂

In order to do justice to checking through these photographs I suggest that you take your pad and construct a table like this:

Case	Is it vandalism by your definition?	Is it normally seen as vandalism?	Type of person involved	Assumed motive
1	Yes	Yes	Kids	Excitement? Frustration?
2	Yes	Yes	Soccer fans	Aggression? Celebration?

Then work through the photographs (1–18) filling in each column in your table.

Figure 8   *Examples of in-text questions from self-instructional materials*

- *Access.* Learners who use self-instructional materials are very often studying part-time and at a distance and their study has to be fitted in with other activities. Like other access devices, in-text questions can form a useful re-entry point for learners who temporarily abandon their studies because of arbitrary time constraints.
- *Revision.* Where in-text questions have been integrated into the text, it is possible for learners to scan the text rapidly, looking only for the in-text questions. The points at which they are unable to provide adequate responses should help to identify the parts of the text that require revision. Linking in-text questions to *objectives* also aids *self-assessment* and *revision*.

How long should ITQs be? They should not be so long as to affect the continuity of the argument and ideally they should form an integral part of the text rather than be an interruption to it. In many situations, then, they should be answerable in a few seconds or a minute or two at the most. If the question is of a kind that it is possible to reflect upon for a very long time, make it clear that you want the learner to think for only a minute, say, and then read on. It is a good rule that whenever you ask learners to perform an activity, you suggest the amount of time you expect them to spend on it.

How difficult should ITQs be? The answer to this can be inferred from the different functions (above) that ITQs fulfil. If you want learners to take an active part in their learning, it is unwise to ask questions that are so easy as to be trivial and that are consequently likely to be ignored. This can lead to learners ignoring later non-trivial ones that might have helped them in their learning. For this reason, it may be useful not only to pose the question, but also to include the rationale for attempting it. It is equally undesirable to ask questions that are so difficult that they are unlikely to reinforce many learners with the sensation of success. Broadly, ITQs should result in most learners thinking hard and coming up with a suitable answer. If you have good reason to ask a very difficult question, let the learners know in advance that it is difficult, give them a time limit, and then discuss not only the answer, but why it is so difficult. Also, take care that questions are explicit (and answerable). Ambiguity and uncertainty cause problems and delays for distance learners who have no one to discuss things with.

How often should you include ITQs? This depends on almost all the variables involved – the learners, the teacher or writer, the subject, the level, the time scale, etc. The nature of the subject being studied has a great effect on the appropriate places, length and frequency for ITQs. In some situations effective teaching can consist of what amounts to little more than a long sequence of in-text questions. In other areas ITQs may be much less frequent; none the less there is an important place for them at most levels in most subjects.

L

laboratory work see *practical work*.

learner-centred describes the approach to teaching or training which designs learning material and *learning experiences* to meet the needs of the learner, rather than those of the teacher, institution or subject matter. A learner-centred approach aims to give learners as much choice as possible in what they do. In designing learning materials this may entail strategies such as planning *objectives* and learning outcomes that will meet learners' needs, allowing for alternative routes through the material, catering for different learning styles and planning open-ended activities which relate to learners' work or life experience.

learner characteristics A variety of information about potential learners that will help you to design effective open learning systems and materials. These characteristics may include:

- demographic factors such as age, sex, occupation (and whether employed), personal handicaps;
- motivational factors such as why they are learning, how a learning programme might relate to their work or lives, their aspirations and reservations about learning;
- learning and subject background factors such as educational history, existing knowledge, relevant experience, preferred learning styles, experience of open or distance learning; and
- resource factors such as when, where and how they will be studying, time available, access to media or other facilities, financial support.

What differences will information of this type make? Some characteristics will influence the starting point of your materials, the level of language you adopt, the style of examples and case studies provided and help you define an appropriate *workload*. Others will suggest the style and level of study advice to be offered in advance of study or to be included within the material. In terms of designing a system, some of these characteristics may help to shape decisions about modes of delivery, use of media, and level and type of learner support. As these tend to be fairly costly parts of any open or distance learning system, sound planning decisions are essential to an eventual cost-effective outcome as well as successful learning outcomes. Before you embark on setting up a system or preparing materials you will certainly want to know the potential numbers of learners, and possibly their geographical distribution. Such data will have considerable bearing on your choices of methods of production, delivery, presentation and support of any learning materials – even to the extent of influencing a decision about going ahead or not!

learner profile is a description of an average potential learner or group of learners based on your knowledge of appropriate *learner characteristics*. In order to design and support an open learning system or to prepare good self-instructional materials, you need to know who your clients are likely to be. Any good teaching or training system will be as individualized as possible but frequently we have to aim our teaching at our idea of a typical learner - an idea that is built up through constant contact with learners. Working in open or distance learning may mean that you have little contact with, and little experience of, the learners or that you are providing learning opportunities for a new target group. What can you do to overcome this? Perhaps you might do the following.

- Come to some preliminary working assumptions on the characteristics of the typical learner, using whatever information and experience happens to be available. You can then base your initial planning on these assumptions.
- Exploit every possible source of feedback to help you further develop your picture of the typical learner and how such a learner might react to your materials or system. (See *developmental testing, feedback*.)

The assumptions you make must provide temporary answers to important questions such as:

- What will your typical learners understand by 'studying' – is it based on recent experience or on long-distant schooldays?
- What study skills are they likely to possess?
- What attitudes and anxieties are they likely to bring to their studies?
- What previous knowledge and relevant experience do they possess? (See *prerequisites*.)
- How much time, and what study conditions, are available to them and what can they be expected to do in this time? (See *workload*.)

In many situations, we can provide tentative answers to these questions quite successfully and modify them later in the light of actual experience. Just occasionally, though, a high *drop-out* rate, bad examination results, or any one of a number of signs of discontent among learners can show that we have misjudged the audience and we should be alert to such signs.

It may help you to write a short description of a typical learner you think you are teaching. Here is one such description:

> She is about 27, left school aged 16 without any examination certificates, is a semi-skilled worker, lives in a small town, is married with two young children, has a radio, television and video recorder and audio-cassette player at home. She is not computer literate. She has access to only a small local library, can afford only a few day's pay each year to buy books or to travel to students' meetings, but wants very much to study further and pass academic or technical examinations, in the hope of getting a better job. She will not be used to studying by herself, will be nervous about being assessed, and may perhaps become a drop-out if her course is not suited to her individual needs or the materials are not interesting and readily accessible.

You might find it interesting to write a similar description of your own learners and even more interesting to compare it with one written by a colleague for the same group of learners. (See also *target audience*.)

learning experiences is a term encompassing all the various things learners will come into contact with during their education. A course is a major learning experience that consists of a number of smaller experiences. Reading a textbook can be a learning experience; so can watching a film, taking a test, doing a written exercise, and performing a laboratory experiment. Even taking a final examination is a learning experience! Some learning experiences, such as lessons, are part of a formal programme; other valuable experiences, such as browsing round the appropriate shelves of a library or talking to fellow learners, may not be programmed at all. (See *activities*.)

If you are *learner-centred* in your approach, you are likely to think of a course as a number of appropriately varied learning experiences, rather than as a body of subject matter – and learning materials that you produce are likely to benefit from this view.

learning manager is anyone charged with some formal responsibility for a learner's progress within a particular system. Learning managers' titles vary from system to system reflecting a variety of responsibilities and the type of education or training being offerred. They may be known as tutors, mentors, supervisors, counsellors, teachers, etc.

learning styles Do learners have different learning styles? And if so, how can, or should, we take this into account in preparing self-instructional materials? Responses to these questions depend largely on what we mean by styles. We know from experience that people learn at different speeds and choose different routes through what they are expected to learn. So, in theory, self-instructional materials should allow for these differences. Most usually, though, they are prepared with some average student in mind, who is allowed a week, perhaps, to complete a unit of work, and is expected to do almost all of what is prescribed. Occasionally the materials include extra remedial work for those likely to have difficulties, or more advanced activities for faster learners.

The term 'learning styles' also covers ways in which learners approach or interact with what has to be learned. Some researchers think there are people who learn best by going from rules to examples and others who should go from examples to rules; to cater for both we need to alternate the approaches in the same material, clearly signalling important rules and examples.

Similarly, researchers think that people can be divided into those who learn holistically, by mastering broad concepts and bodies of knowledge as a whole, and those who learn serially, working through details one after another until they have mastered all. Again we need to provide for both styles. A concept map or contents list, for example, offers holistic learners an overall view of some learning material, while serial learners may prefer to start reading it through.

Other researchers have shown that each medium teaches learners to acquire particular sets of codes. Thus learners from television or video pick up, through watching, learning styles that incorporate unconscious responses to, say, a zoom on to a face or an object. Professional producers of television use these codes, for instance, to emphasize particular points or to create emotional effects, and experienced viewers respond to them more than naive viewers.

Other sets of codes apply to other media. When the codes are ignored, learners experienced in using these media can be put off, partly because they perceive the materials, whether on television, audio-tape or in print, as amateurish, but also because they cannot pick up the extra meaning.

Additionally, you find learners referred to as surface-level or deep-level processors, convergers or divergers, assimilators or accommodators, activists, theorists, pragmatists or reflectors. All these descriptions of approaches to learning have implications for the way such people would like learning materials to be designed. Usually the best we can do is to use a variety of approaches or *styles*, and media in order to suit a range of different kinds of learner.

learning workshop This is usually a description of a physical location where learners have access to the materials, resources, equipment and support necessary for a module, course or programme of study. Such workshops are used particularly in further education and adult basic education where they may concentrate on a particular subject area, such as a maths workshop, and for vocational and non-vocational learning and assessment in industrial training. A well-designed and supported learning workshop system allows the possibility of considerable learner autonomy and opportunities for development of an individual flexible-learning programme.

As well as providing resources and support, learning workshops maintain records of usage, offer assessment opportunities and keep learner progress data. You may also find them referred to as open learning workshops, drop-in centres/workshops, open access centres or flexible-learning centres.

M

maintenance see *course presentation and monitoring*.

marking is a term that is applied to some of the processes used for learner *assessment.* One process results in some kind of numerical score or standard grade being awarded for the work, a process sometimes known as *summative* assessment or evaluation. Another kind of process, *formative* assessment, aims to produce useful comments on the learner's work (see *feedback*). The two processes often merge into one, as, for example, when a teacher writes something like '75% – if your diagram had shown more detail you would have done even better'.

In any form of education, marking poses a number of problems and these are particularly difficult when you are able to meet your learners only rarely. In open and distance learning it is important that marking should be constructive, that it should happen at regular intervals, that it should be to some extent standardized (see *monitoring*) and that it should be academically (or otherwise professionally) acceptable.

To say that marking should be constructive is to imply that it should be formative – helpful to the learner and part of the teaching/learning process – whether or not a summative score or grade has to be arrived at. *Distance learners* cannot expect to receive the amount of *feedback* that is regularly available to institution-based learners, so full use must be made of these opportunities to pass on useful comments and suggestions, which may be the only responsive teaching that distance learners receive. Comments need to be carefully and tactfully phrased because learners may well be short of emotional and moral support in their studies and are likely to be sensitive to criticism, particularly if they see it as being destructive rather than constructive. Comments should supplement, but not contradict, the estimate of their progress that learners have formed through *self-assessment* which means that at least some of the self-assessed exercises and activities in the materials should, if possible, be broadly comparable in standard with any *tutor-marked assignments* or *computer-marked assignments* which are set.

Learners should not normally go too long without receiving the teaching feedback which a marked assignment can give. Assignments should therefore be required at regular intervals. This is sometimes known as ***continuous assessment*** (as opposed to a simple end-of-course test) although in fact it is intermittent rather than continuous. Just how frequent it should be will clearly depend to some extent on the nature of the subject and the course. There are other reasons, too, why a regular pattern of marked assignments is desirable. It is not only learners who need feedback about their progress – you, as the teacher or course provider, also need this if you are to check that all is well with the learners, with the teaching and with the course as a whole. A regular assignment pattern can help to influence your learners to organize their studies sensibly and not fall too far behind if they have to meet a fixed finishing target such as an ***examination***.

The main aim of marking then, apart from the production of a summative grading of some kind, is to help the learner. In making comments tactfully and aiming them at the learner as an individual, some general indication of the standard that is required should also be given. Distance learners have little opportunity to compare themselves with fellow-learners and they have to rely on self-assessment and a tutor's marking to give them an idea of their relative standing. If grades given to learners for continuous assessment are (as sometimes happens) very different from their performance under the controlled conditions of a final examination, they are entitled to complain that, for some reason or another, they have been misled. In any case, if the required standard is blurred too much, the professional reputation or academic acceptability of the course or institution may suffer. Self-assessment, continuous assessment, and examination results, although not identical in purpose, present different aspects of the same picture. Constructive and consistent marking can help to ensure that they do.

media choice/media mix

In planning self-instructional materials we sometimes have to choose between alternative media through which to present our teaching. Although a good deal of attention has been given to this kind of decision-making, the choice is often relatively easy to make in practice because for much of the time, local constraints, questions of accessibility and of cost virtually dictate the media through which we have to work. Even if a genuine choice does exist it is very rarely a critical one – you do not need to know very much about education or training to realize that the same things have been, are being, and are likely to go on being taught quite successfully in many different ways using many different media. The converse is also true – poor teaching is likely to be produced by poor teachers whatever media they use, and the most sophisticated high technology devices are in themselves no guarantee of high quality.

This does not mean, of course, that all media are of equal potential for all teaching purposes, or that we should not be careful to make the best of whatever choice we have. What is best for us and our own particular approach may not necessarily be the best for anyone else. As in all other aspects of planning teaching it is up to each of us to make our own decision, bearing in mind the characteristics of the media from which we have to choose – and possibly working within the requirements and budget of our institution or client, any house style, and limitations on production facilities. We can all agree, for example, that film and *video* can provide lively illustrations of things actually working, but need not agree as to their usefulness in any one specific instance. And we can all agree that it is useful to incorporate a certain amount of variety in self-instructional materials without all selecting the same media for the same things. Some of the media available are shown in Figure 9.

There are three very important considerations that should influence all media choices:

- Educational effectiveness
- Accessibility to the learners
- Cost-effectiveness.

We can exercise some control over the educational effectiveness of whatever media we select because it depends to a large extent upon our skill as teachers. Problems of accessibility and cost-effectiveness may be outside our control, however, and may limit our choice to an available sub-set of media possibilities.

Accessibility is vitally important to any learners who have to use self-instructional materials. The great advantage of this mode of learning is that learners can choose the time, the place and the duration of each period of study to suit themselves. Ideally they should be able to do this no matter what media we decide to use. Does our particular choice make this possible? Is it easy ('user-friendly') for them to use?

Compared with other media, text is not only highly accessible, but highly portable and very much under the learners' control. Learners with just a few minutes to spare can pick up a book and make good use of the time to study one small, easily-located section; they would be unlikely to attempt to do the same with any electronic device. Other media depend on some sort of technical device ('hardware') in order to produce the message, and some also need other people to be available at the same time if we include things under the 'human interaction' grouping (See Figure 9). Even if learners have their own hardware, they are very much restricted by its portability and the study conditions it demands. Commuters regularly study their written materials

Some of the media available in open learning

Print

- o Books, pamphlets, etc—already published, or specially written
- o Specially written "wrap around" study guides to already published material
- o Specially written self-teaching texts, e.g. "tutorials-in-print"
- o Workbooks for use along with audiotape or videotape, CBT, practical work, etc
- o Self-tests, project guides, notes on accreditation requirements, bibliographies, etc
- o Maps, charts, photographs, posters, etc
- o Material from newspapers, journals and periodicals
- o Handwritten materials passing between learners and tutor.

Audio-visual

- o Audio-cassettes/discs/CDs
- o Radio broadcasts
- o Slides or filmstrip
- o Film or film loops
- o Video-cassettes
- o Television broadcasts
- o Computer based training —CBT
- o Interactive video.

Practical or project work

- o Materials, equipment, specimens for learner's own use—e.g. home experiment kits, keyboards, official forms
- o Field-work or other use of learner's local environment— e.g. observation, interviews, collection of evidence, etc

- o Projects in local offices, farms, workshops, etc
- o Assignments based on learner's workplace

Human interaction

At-a-distance

- o Telephone conversation between learner and tutor (supplementing written communications)
- o Learner-learner telephone conversations
- o Several learners in telephone contact at the same time, with or without a tutor, by means of a "conference call"
- o Video conferencing
- o Computer conferencing.

Face-to-face

- o Learners' self-help groups
- o Help from line managers/ "mentors"/technicians/others
- o Occasional seminars, tutorials, lectures by tutors or other group organizers
- o One-day, one week, weekend, or other short group sessions (residential or otherwise).

Others? (What?)

- o
- o
- o
- o

Figure 9 *Some of the media available in open learning (from Rowntree, 1992)*

during their journeys to work, and can make use of personal *audio*-cassette players in similar circumstances but it would be impossible to study from a video recording or film while travelling on public transport. Photographic transparencies are excellent when projected, but they are much less effective when you have to use a relatively primitive hand viewer. However good your media components, there is a cost if they require the learner to go to the machine – and machines need maintenance. If your firm or institution has its own facilities and technical back-up, so much the better, but even then the individual learners are often constrained by having to make a booking at a place and time that they would not have chosen. If you can combine any regular *tutorial-support* sessions with media access, your learners will at least get double value for being temporarily unable to decide the time and place for themselves.

Repeatability is another important consideration. Can the learner go back to a point that has not been understood and go over it again and again if necessary? It is easy to do this with text – if you wanted to, you could go back to the beginning of this entry in a matter of seconds. It takes longer for the learner to do the same thing with an audio or video cassette. Computer-based learning scores highly on ease of repeatability but broadcast *television* and *radio* are problematic unless the learner has suitable recording equipment.

Any requirement for hardware places a constraint upon the learner. This means that whenever we plan to use a media component, we need to strike a balance between the costs and benefits to the learner. There are also costs to us, the teachers, and to our organization. Any time and money which we spend, and which in turn our learners have to spend, on the media, represent resources that might have been spent elsewhere. We should be aware of this 'opportunity cost'. There is also the question of cost-effectiveness. Are we getting the educational effectiveness that we are paying for? Do we need high quality material, or can we compromise with something less expensive? We also need to be aware of the novelty or fashion factor when looking at potential uses of new media. Developing effective learning materials for a novel teaching medium is time-consuming and expensive. Committing oneself to the use of a developing medium can lead to expensive mistakes. Unless it is your particular research area or your institution has vast resources it may be wise to leave it until it has been tried and tested by someone else.

In summary, we should select our media so as to exploit their particular advantages. We should be aware that we are imposing costs of various kinds on our learners, ourselves and our organizations, and make sure that the benefits are commensurate with the costs.

modules/modular structure As in other modes of learning and teaching, self-instructional materials have to be subdivided into pieces of more or less standard length. These might be called lessons, units or whatever is appropriate and their length may be determined by some unit of study time, say the amount of time a learner might reasonably spend studying in a week. The term 'module' is used in a variety of ways, but usually means a sequence of lessons in one single topic (amounting in themselves to at least a mini-course) that can be combined in various ways with other modules to constitute one particular study programme. Thus a learner who is studying a number of modules on psychology may first of all study a module on elementary statistics; a learner who has selected a number of modules on economics may also include the same standard statistics module.

Modular structures can vary from the simple to the extremely complex. In some cases learners can have complete freedom to select one module from group A say, one module from group B, and one from group C. This is sometimes known as 'a cafeteria system'! Often, however, there are restrictions on the choices available to the learner. The reasons are usually one or more of the following:

- To ensure that each learner includes at least the minimum amount of what are thought to be essential background subjects, eg at least one of the mathematics modules.
- To ensure that learners' individual combinations of modules add up to what the course providers feel to be reasonably coherent pieces of study, especially if they are being accredited.
- To restrict certain combinations of somewhat similar modules where learners might to some extent be getting credit twice for some of their studies, eg where 'Survey Research' overlaps 'Market Research'.

There are clear advantages to learners if they are able to design their own courses by selecting the modules most relevant to their needs. There are also clear advantages to the teachers and the organization if there is no unnecessary duplication of work. The disadvantage can be that, in attempting to design, say, an elementary statistics module for general use by learners with a variety of goals, you may have to make compromises that result in a module that is not quite right for anyone.

monitoring In an open or distance learning system which employs a large number of, probably, part-time and geographically dispersed tutorial, counselling or mentoring staff, monitoring can refer to the systems employed to ensure the quality of support offered to learners. We need to endeavour to provide equivalent stimulus, experience and *assessment* for each learner no matter where they are or who is responsible for their support. Tutors may be monitored for the effectiveness of their correspondence teaching, the consistency and comparability of their grading, or for whatever other functions they fulfil.

Monitoring may also refer to the process of checking the effectiveness of the learning material or course. (See *course presentation and monitoring, evaluation*.)

motivation If learners are motivated, they will approach their studies willingly, perhaps even with a certain amount of pleasure. A psychologist might say that motivation is concerned with the encouragement of goal-directed behaviour, but however it is described, motivation is normally something that is highly valued. Good teachers always aim to foster, enhance and perhaps diversify whatever has motivated their learners to commit themselves to the job of learning.

How does high motivation come about? In several ways, perhaps because:

- learners finds the desired activity is satisfying in itself, eg they enjoy solving problems or playing the piano;
- although the activity itself is not specially enjoyable, learners are successful at it and the boost to their self-regard is reward enough;
- succeeding at the desired activity holds out the promise of some future reward, eg a certificate leading to a good job; or
- conversely, failing at the desired activity will incur some sort of penalty, eg no certificate, no job.

The first two are sometimes known as 'intrinsic motivation', because the motivation comes from within the individual. 'Extrinsic motivation', the latter two, comes from the hope of rewards or the fear of penalties, from outside the individual. Motivation in most people is often a mixture of these. It is quite possible at one and the same time to enjoy learning more about computer programming, to relish other people's admiration for your growing expertise, to hope that your firm will promote you if you do really well, and to worry about what might happen if you don't.

Any learning that is done in the hope of acquiring a certificate or qualification of some kind is extrinsically motivated because gaining the certificate will be a reward for the learner, while failing to get it will usually be penalty enough in itself, quite apart from any other sanctions. Nevertheless, it is a matter of everyday experience that not all learners who are studying for the award of a certificate are therefore automatically highly motivated and that intrinsic motivation can be both more powerful and more durable.

How can we encourage intrinsic motivation through our design of self-instructional materials? The most important thing is to get learners to identify themselves personally with the learning process. If learners see the *objectives* as worthwhile things in themselves and they understand why these objectives are important, they are likely to adopt them as their own. The *overview* or *advance organizers* at the beginning of each section of material should also provide their own kind of rationale on the lines of, 'This is what we're going to be talking about, and this is what you'll be able to do by the end of the unit.' If we include plenty of *activities* in our materials and give learners good reasons for these activities, they will want to attempt them. The act of *self-assessment* is also connected closely with motivation – learners who test themselves are taking personal responsibility for at least part of their own education and are more likely to identify with it.

multiple-choice questions see *objective tests* and *computer-marked assignments.*

N

National Vocational Qualifications (NVQs) A recent review of the UK system of vocational qualifications recommended that such qualifications should relate more directly and clearly to competence required in work and that they should be statements of outcomes defined in terms of occupational standards. A new system of National Vocational Qualifications being formed under the aegis of the National Council for Vocational Qualifications are based on a statement of *competence* incorporating units of competence containing elements of competence and their associated performance criteria. The accreditation of NVQs calls for competence-based assessment of *work-based learning*.

non-verbal cues Human speech, and hence all face-to-face teaching, is normally accompanied by non-verbal cues that are highly significant. Whenever we talk to other people, we send out a stream of information over and above the actual words we use. Because of this, a verbatim transcript of a lecture, for example, conveys less than the actual lecturer did; it cannot convey the speaker's tone of voice, facial expression or body posture. These and other non-verbal cues send out powerful messages of their own to emphasize, moderate or alter the meaning of what is being said. In the extreme case, the words spoken can be completely contradicted by the non-verbal cues, and the listeners are left in no doubt that the speaker is being ironic or perhaps sarcastic.

Whether consciously or not, we all send out non-verbal cues when we are teaching in a face-to-face situation. If the non-verbal cues are missing, as in written learning materials, or much filtered, as in *audio* or *video* components, distance learners are likely to receive a very diluted kind of teaching unless positive steps are taken to replace the missing signals. Face-to-face learners may, for example, be quick to detect, because of the tutor's tone of voice and emphatic manner, that topic A is the really important one, no matter what the course description may say. This revelation of the hidden curriculum is denied to distance learners who will need a more accurate, more detailed, and perhaps more honest description of what their priorities should be.

Many of the messages that non-verbal cues convey are evaluative. The words may be factual and neutrally stressed, but the signals may be saying things like, 'This principle is important'; 'This book need not be read very carefully'; 'This writer is suspect'; 'This is a particularly stupid kind of error and I intend to penalise it'; or even, 'This hasn't been satisfactorily worked out, and I can't understand it myself'.

How can we help distance learners, who cannot receive most of these messages? Our own awareness is perhaps the most important thing, for it is only when we fully appreciate what can easily be lost when we commit our teaching to paper or to tape that we begin to give the fully explicit argument or description that distance learners need. This may mean that we have to spell our priorities out consciously and fully for the first time, and not leave it to the inspiration of the moment to produce the appropriate cues. For many reasons, such a full spelling-out is needed anyway, whenever we are preparing self-instructional materials.

norm-referenced assessment When we assess learners, we need some standard against which to measure them. If we judge them not on some pre-determined standard, nor against their own previous achievements, but against the standard set by their fellow-students, we are using norm-referenced assessment. (See also *criterion-referenced assessment*.)

Norm-referenced assessment can take a number of forms. A simple form might be to use assessment results to describe learners as 'average', 'above average', and 'below average'. If the word average refers to the mean score obtained on the test(s), then any individual learner's result clearly depends upon on how fellow learners have performed. It is easy to see that in one group of learners a score of, say, 60 per cent might result in a below-average grading, while with less gifted learners the same score could qualify as an above-average grading. This seems unfair to most people and the impression of unfairness remains, no matter how much the actual scoring is shrouded in statistical language such as defining the 'below average' score as two standard deviations below the arithmetic mean.

Of course all assessment, in the last resort, is norm-referenced in some way. When we fix the pass level in advance we may not be basing our gradings on the actual performance of the learner group that is being tested, but where do we get the pre-determined 'absolute' standards that we claim to be using? They are usually based on our own experience of what is a reasonable standard to expect, which means that we are really measuring this group of learners against some notional average performance observed by us in previous learner groups – a method that you could argue is every bit as norm-referenced as measuring against this group's average score.

While we might philosophically find out-and-out norm-referencing unacceptable, some degree of norm-referencing can be very convenient to teachers. An unvarying pass rate from year to year prevents the heated accusations of over-severe marking that arise whenever the pass rate takes a dive. It avoids a sudden drop in the grades achieved by learners (as opposed to the raw scores on which they were based) which could be used to evaluate, and perhaps thereby to criticize, the teaching. Moreover, if you have a number of tutors teaching on the same course, the problem of getting them all to use the same standards when marking learners' assignments can (apparently) be easily solved by telling them to award 5 per cent As, 20 per cent Bs, 50 per cent Cs and so on. This can be moderated by allowing tutors to award more high gradings if they can prove that they really do have an exceptional proportion of well-prepared learners or high fliers. This kind of 'marking on the curve', that fits the scores into some sort of standard distribution, clearly has a number of administrative and political advantages to offer.

O

objective tests are designed to assess knowledge or skill without requiring the marker to exercise any judgement. They can be marked and graded by a computer, or by anyone who has the 'correct' answers. A test should consist of at least 20 items if it is to be valid; some tests have more than 100 items. Objective tests are particularly suitable for use in self-instructional materials. They allow a learner to take a test whenever it suits them without needing to refer to a specialist tutor. Objective tests are also a very cost-effective way of providing assessment opportunities for distance learners especially if there are large numbers involved. They also allow for coverage of the content of a course where other forms of *assessment* may have to be selective about the knowledge and skills assessed. However, as in any form of teaching, it is best to include a variety of forms of assessment.

The most usual form of objective test question or item is the multiple-choice question. Each item consists of a stem, which asks the question, and a set of several options from which the correct answer is selected. The incorrect options are known as distractors. For example:

STEM		In which unit could you measure the rate of change of an electric charge?
DISTRACTOR	A	coulomb
DISTRACTOR	B	watt
CORRECT OPTION	C	ampere
DISTRACTOR	D	joule

It is possible to have stems which ask for more than one correct answer and then you need a correspondingly higher number of distractors.

Composing good test items calls for a certain amount of skill and improves with practice. The chief difficulties are finding an adequate number of plausible but incorrect distractors and avoiding clues in the construction of the question. Objective test items should always be tried out before being used in earnest. Colleagues can check them for clarity and accuracy and some form of *developmental testing* will show you how learners react to them.

One advantage of using objective tests is that you can use statistical item analysis to check results for each of the items. The facility index for an item is the percentage of correct responses, and indicates the level of difficulty of the item. A low facility index indicates that the item is too hard for your learners or is unclear in some way. A high facility index indicates that the item is too easy for your learners, contains a give-away and/or depends only on common sense.

The discrimination index for an item is the correlation between the scores on the item alone and the total scores. That is to say, if learners who score high on the test as a whole tend to score high on an item, that item will have a high discrimination index. A low discrimination means that the item may be wrong or unclear, or may not be measuring the same ability as the rest of the test. Item analysis cannot tell you what is wrong, but it can tell you which items need to be looked at again. Once you do this the fault may be fairly obvious.

Objective tests have several other advantages. They offer a quick and reliable method of sampling large fields of knowledge at medium-to-low cognitive levels. They may be self-administered, possibly via a computer terminal. They are quick and easy to mark and are suitable for *self-assessment.* They minimize problems for learners with writing and/or self-expression difficulties. They help diagnosis of learner errors so that learners can be advised or re-routed. They can also pinpoint weaknesses in the learning materials.

On the other hand they are not easy or quick to set. In particular, the wording of items on topics in which there are few clear-cut answers requires considerable skill. They cannot test higher cognitive levels, including power of originality and self-expression. If the only form of assessment is objective testing, teachers may bias their teaching and learners their learning towards what is most easily tested. These tests cannot detect whether learners are guessing or getting the right answer for the wrong reasons.

Although 'one from several' multiple-choice questions are used more frequently than any other type, there are many other ways in which objective test items may be presented. You can, for instance, ask learners to put items (eg strengths of acids) into the correct order. You can have a number of options in the stem (eg names of countries) as well as in the alternative answers (eg different export crops) and ask learners to match the one with the other. You can present a diagram (eg a time-base circuit) as the stem together with a choice of interpretations (eg the resultant wave-form). You can supply a set of statements together with a set of reasons and ask learners to identify those statements and reasons that are correct in themselves and then to match the statements to reasons. In subjects where few answers are either uniquely or 100 per cent 'correct' you can use forms of wording such as 'which is generally conceded to be . . .?' or 'In the opinion of most critics at the time . . .?' or, 'What is one commonly used form of treatment . . .?'

Presenting different forms of test item in this way can add a good deal of interest and variety to tests. But we need to beware of making the structure and wording of an item so complex that we test the learners' comprehension of the test item rather than of the subject matter itself.

objectives Educational objectives are usually statements designed to identify as clearly as possible what learners should do, or be able to do, in order to demonstrate that they have learnt something. Why do we need objectives? Because if we want to know whether we are teaching success-fully, we need to have a clear perception of what is to be achieved.

There are many advantages in expressing objectives in terms of the know-ledge, skills, values and beliefs that we hope learners will acquire during the learning process. We are not able, directly, to observe the accumulation of knowledge or the acquisition of values specified by our objectives, since these are internalized by each learner. We can, however, look for evidence of them by observing the ways in which learners behave. For this reason educational objectives are stated as far as possible in terms of what learners should be able to do at the end of the learning process. This is particularly important in *distance learning*.

Broad statements of intent are usually known as *aims*, and are often expressed in terms of what the teacher intends to do, rather than what the learner should ultimately be able to do. For example:

> The aim of this course is to explain the nature of science and the way in which scientific knowledge accumulates.

But, of course, this could equally well be expressed in learner terms:

> On completion of this course you should have an understanding of the nature of science and the way in which scientific knowledge accumulates.

Aims such as these may be used in a number of ways. They may be used by course planners, not only as a way of exchanging ideas, but also as a basis from which more specific statements of intent can be developed. Equally, they may be used to give learners a general idea of the course. The problem with aims which use words like 'understand' is that they do not specify what learners are to do in order to demonstrate that they understand. It is likely that you will find that you want to declare your intentions more precisely by using verbs that state what a learner is to do (list, describe, explain, etc) rather than 'understand' or 'know' which refer to something inside the learner's head. These rather more specific statements of intent are usually known as objectives.

The following is an example of the way in which a fairly specific statement of objectives can be used to clarify a broadly expressed aim:

> The overall aim of this unit has been to help you make the first step in understanding how science works. This is why we have chosen everyday observations as the factual material and for our discussion. Having studied this unit you should appreciate how a simple scientific model is derived from observations, how predictions can be made on the basis of the model, and how and why such predictions are tested by new observations.
>
> Some more specific aspects of this overall aim are listed below as more detailed objectives. You should be able to:
>
> 1. Describe the motion of the Earth around the Sun.
> 2. Describe the motion of the Moon with respect to the Earth and the Sun.
> 3. Give reasons for local variations of the seasonal cycle.
> 4. Give reasons for the phases of the Moon.
>   Etc, etc.

Different teachers starting from the same aim might well produce a somewhat different set of objectives, but the important point is that this particular writer has tried to make clear to the learners what they are expected to do on completing their studies.

It can be argued that there is still some vagueness in the statements of objectives; that it would be possible for different teachers observing the same learners to disagree about whether a given learner had achieved a particular objective. Consequently, some people have advocated even more precise statements of objectives, suggesting that they should identify the required behaviour, the required level of performance, and the conditions under which it is to be done. An example of this type of objective is:

> Given any 10 groupings of any 4 single digit numbers which may be positive or negative (conditions applicable), the learner should be able to compute the sum of each group (behaviour to be exhibited), obtaining at least 8 of the 10 summations within a period of 5 minutes (level of performance to be achieved).

Such objectives, often known as 'behavioural objectives', have been widely adopted in both education and training programmes.

The problem with these types of objectives is that in order to reduce ambiguity they are expressed in very narrow terms, and as such often identify very limited, and at times trivial, aspects of learning. The simple arithmetical example shown above is at a very low and mechanical level (despite the level of language used to express it!). Attempts to deal with broader, less trivial issues, usually lead to general statements of intent which are much less precise.

One way of improving such objectives is to link them to sample questions or test items that define more closely what the learner has to do. Most learners (and most teachers) find they can get a better idea of what they have to do by looking at past examination questions rather than syllabuses or published aims.

All learners, and especially *distance or open learners* working on their own with self-instructional materials, should have some idea of what is expected of them before they start work in earnest. A statement of objectives would seem to be a particularly clear way of doing this. In practice, however, a list of detailed objectives can be a very dull way of introducing a topic. There are better ways of doing this (eg *overviews*). In some cases, such as where important new terminology is to be introduced, defined and discussed, learners will not even be able to understand the objectives until after they have studied the relevant materials. It is often best to provide the learner with statements of objectives as checklists at fairly frequent intervals after the study has taken place, and to include some sample test items as a further clarification. If you include *post-tests* in your materials, your learners will automatically have a set of sample questions.

Objectives are useful for teachers as well as for learners. In the planning stages of materials production they provide a relatively clear and unambiguous way for teachers to communicate their intentions to one another. This is particularly important when a group of people are working together to produce a course or a set of learning materials. Later on objectives can also be used to monitor learner progress, and to diagnose ways in which the learning materials need to be improved.

Objectives may also be referred to as learning outcomes (see also *competence*).

open learning/open learning systems are terms describing a wide range of learning opportunities that aim both to assist learners in gaining better access to knowledge and skills they might otherwise be denied and to give learners the optimum degree of control over their own learning. The two major elements of a successful approach to open learning are the removal of barriers, such as physical location and timing of courses and formal entry requirements, which may prevent individuals from taking advantage of learning opportunities; and the importance of focusing on the needs of individual learners rather than on the requirements of institutional structures. A *learner-centred* approach would concentrate on such things as location to suit the learner (eg home, workplace, local centre or a combination of these); availability of courses or programmes when they are needed; length of study or training which depends on an individual's pace of learning, and on attainment of the required knowledge or *competences*; a programme negotiated to suit the needs of learners rather than a fixed menu of courses for groups of sufficient size; use of a variety of teaching and learning styles; and provision of *tutorial support* and a system of *assessment* and *evaluation*.

The main features of open learning systems are likely to be some combination of multi-media *packages*, *learning workshops*, *counselling* and *tutorial support*, modularization of courses, flexible timetabling, a negotiated curriculum and support through guidance. Such systems are also often referred to as *flexible learning*.

overviews An overview is a summary of a lesson, module, etc, presented to the learner very early in the learning experience to which it relates. It should give learners as accurate an idea as possible of what is to come, so as to prepare them, orient them, and it is to be hoped, motivate them. It is one example of an *advance organizer*. *Aims* and *objectives* are other examples.

Self-instructional material often begins and ends with a *summary*. The difference between overviews and final summaries is, fairly obviously, that learners have completed the main part of their study before meeting the final summary, so they are able to use the new terminology and principles that they have met and have been practising.

A good summary should not only summarize the lesson in words that the incoming learner can understand; it may also very usefully indicate the relationship of the lesson to the rest of the course so far and, like the objectives, describe where the learners are going and what they will be able to do. Here is an example:

> You have already learnt to fix your boat's position visually during daylight and, by using lighthouses and other lights, at night. In this lesson you will learn how to use radio beacons in order to fix your position in fog and at night when you cannot see any identifiable light. You will also learn the limitations of this technique and the problems it sometimes presents.

A good overview thus tells the learners where they have been, where they are now, and not only where they are going but why they are going there.

P

pacing A basic tenet of open and distance learning is that learners have the opportunity to learn at their own pace. However, there are situations when that flexibility is constrained, perhaps within the framework of an external *examination* system and learners appreciate an element of pacing to help them to meet an examination date. One helpful thing is to break the materials into chunks, units or blocks which can be studied in a day, a week or a month so that learners can see roughly where they need to be by when, given how fast or slowly they each work through the materials. The need to submit assignments regularly helps learners to pace themselves as do some fixed-time elements of the package such as tutorials, work-based experience or TV and radio broadcasts.

packages A package is an assembly of a number of separate pieces of learning material ('components') on a given subject or topic. We often add some kind of descriptive word to packages so that we talk about learning packages, revision packages, remedial packages, multi-media packages, etc. Learning packages are fundamental to open and distance learning systems.

Where you have a very long, but nevertheless essentially single piece of learning material, it may be advantageous to the learner to separate into a number of instalments so that there is an increase in the number of built-in *access devices*. Apart from this, however, there should be some rationale for maintaining the separate identity of each component of a package, and if it is a multi-media package you should be able to justify, on pedagogical grounds, the media that you have chosen for the separate components. (See *media choice*.) The larger and more complex the package, the greater the number of problems it may present. Most of these problems are concerned with integration or with getting the components ready on time.

In the ideal learning package, the whole should be greater than the sum of the parts, for each component should not only do its own job, but also help to illuminate the rest of the package. Each component should have its own objectives that contribute to the overall objectives, and also objectives that relate to the integration of the package as a whole. If each component is to be prepared by a different person, it is helpful to have someone who is to take responsibility for this overall integration. If you do not, you will lose opportunities for crosslinking/referencing, which is a valuable aspect of teaching. Without this, you may produce a set of largely unrelated components that can produce confused (and even contradictory) impressions in the learner's mind.

One way of helping learners to integrate packages is to use *study guides*. A good study guide can help the learner to select a personal path through the different components of the package and offer guidance as to the significance of the package as whole. Some packages achieve the same result by making the first component an *overview* of the complete package, with the final component putting forward a synthesis of all the components that have gone before.

To arrange your learning materials into packages can help the learners by adding some variety to their educational experiences, by giving them easier access to different points in the learning process, and by catering for different learning styles. Packages do not necessarily have to be multi-media ones; very effective and interesting packages have been assembled from a skilful mixture of different types of written material.

people with disabilities may want to use your open or distance learning system and materials. Some of them enrol in open or distance teaching schemes because they feel it will be easier for them than face-to-face education; others do so because they have no real alternative, but many enrol for the same reasons as anyone else, irrespective of their handicap. In terms of distance learning, we can think of disabilities of three kinds:

- Some learners have physical handicaps that make it very difficult for them to participate in conventional education; those in wheelchairs or with severe mobility problems. They can participate in distance education, however, if the handicap does not affect their ability to read, write, watch television, etc. You may need to suggest alternative activities for such people if your course involves fieldwork, physical activity, or access to public buildings for research purposes, etc.

- Some have handicaps that do not directly affect their work but do affect their efficiency as people and therefore as learners. People suffering from epilepsy, migraine or other pain find that at times study is very difficult. You cannot take this kind of disability into account when designing learning materials, although of course tutors or mentors can be expected to do so.

- The most serious handicaps for learners taking part in open or distance education directly interfere with their use of material or their participation.

Blind or partially sighted, deaf or partially hearing, those who cannot write or use a word processor, and those with language handicaps such as dyslexia fall into this category. They may have difficulties reading. Many such learners have to go to a great deal of trouble arranging access to the materials at all, whether through friends who read and write for them, through using Braille or tape, or through some other means. They may have to pay a great deal for special equipment or to helpers. Participating in open or distance education may be at great cost to themselves in many ways. Tutors, counsellors and mentors will need to be alerted to the needs of such learners.

Probably the most important thing to remember as you prepare learning materials and devise a learning system is that disabled learners are individuals, like all the others, and they must be judged academically as such. Commonly they are highly-motivated and produce high-quality work. Thinking through the accessibility of your system and materials to such people may cause you to reflect on what 'open' means for your learners.

peer support usually refers to the ways in which learners can support and help each other with their learning problems. (See *distance learners* and *self-help groups*.)

piloting see *developmental testing*.

post-test As its name implies, this is a test that follows a lesson or other learning experience. It is usually intended to test whether the learning has been satisfactory. It is often an important feature of self-instructional materials since it is the chief way in which open and distance learners can tell whether they have mastered the work.

Where adequate *objectives* have been formulated, there is not normally much doubt about the form a post-test should take. Objectives usually tell us what the learner will be able to do after studying the lesson/module etc, and the test consists of asking the learner to do just that. For example:

OBJECTIVE – You will be able to use a prismatic compass in good visibility to measure the bearing of any given landmark to an accuracy of plus or minus 2 degrees.
POST-TEST – Ask learners to do it.

This is sometimes called a 'criterion' test because it is applying a clearly-defined and predetermined standard. Note that the objective not only effectively determines the nature of the post-test, but indicates the conditions in which it is to be attempted. If you are working in a technical field where knowledge and skills can be closely defined, it is possible to arrive at a very clear idea of what you have to teach and hence what you need to test.

Not all objectives, however, are immediately or directly testable. Some objectives, and many *aims*, are concerned with the long-term behaviour or attitudes of the student, and you cannot easily defer the post-test for several years. Some objectives may be concerned with skills and behaviours in specific situations that cannot realistically be reproduced for test purposes. In some teaching and learning situations, especially at the higher levels and where creativity is involved, it may indeed be impossible to devise objectives that are precise enough to specify the kind of post-test that would establish whether or not they have been attained.

If you are not operating in the climate of precision where post-tests are indicated by the objectives, it is possible to use the post-test to assess more than mastery of the lesson which the learner has just completed. If the post-test proper is not unduly long or complicated, it is sometimes possible to add a few items of a revisionary nature that stretch back further than the immediate lesson. It is also possible to add items that test the *prerequisites* needed for the learner's next lesson, ie the kind of test items that are found in *pre-tests*. If you do this, the combined post- and pre-test becomes a single vital link between one lesson and the next.

Bear in mind that post-tests are also *access devices* that can be particularly useful for *revision* purposes. Your learners should be able to go through their materials, picking out the post-tests without difficulty and using them to decide whether or not the lesson to which they refer is one that needs to be looked at again.

practical work The inclusion, in open or distance learning materials, of practical work, laboratory work, or workshop experience of the 'What happens if we . . .?' kind, sounds like a daunting if not impossible task. It can be done, however, by selecting a suitable combination of several possible ways. Some methods are fairly expensive in terms of equipment or facilities and most are costly in both preparation and study time, but good practical work, or an acceptable substitute, can be a very stimulating part of a distance-teaching process.

First be sure that you really need practical work. Are you doing it because it is a much respected tradition, or have you arrived at some explicit *aims* and *objectives* that cannot be achieved by some other means? Among the aims attributed to this kind of work are:

- Mastering the use of standard equipment and measuring techniques.
- Reinforcing the teaching of theory.

- Teaching topics not covered elsewhere.
- Stimulating and maintaining interest and **motivation**, especially in a practically-based subject area.

Many of these can be achieved by means other than working on-site in a custom-built environment.

If it is necessary to provide full-blown practical experience on special equipment for your learners, you can do it by bringing them together for short intensive periods of study of anything from a day to a week. This could be done either within your own organization or by using the facilities, including perhaps the **tutorial support**, available in other places that are geographically convenient to your learners. Alternatively, places like field studies centres and certain further education institutions may already be offering suitable ready-made experiences of one kind or another. Learners whose jobs are in the subject area which they are studying may well have suitable facilities in their place of work (and may already have achieved the practical objectives in terms of skills).

However, all experimental work does not have to be done in the custom-built environment of a workshop or laboratory. Learners can do useful practical work at home, using things readily to hand such as kitchen utensils, household chemicals, garden plants, and the technological devices now found in many homes. They may not always be able to do detailed quantitative work in this way, but much is learned by seeing what happens and predicting or measuring order of magnitude effects. Learners can do even more if you supply them with relatively simple equipment and specimens such as hand lenses, circuit boards with electronic components, electrical multimeters, rock samples, stop watches, etc. Look for items that are small and robust and travel well. It may be cost-effective to allow learners to keep such inexpensive equipment. More expensive items of equipment can be loaned and returned but this needs maintenance, storage and administrative support, the recurring costs of which can outstrip the original capital cost.

Even more so than in the conventional situation, learners doing practical work at home will need comprehensive instructions. They are unlikely to have anyone to consult when carrying out the activities, although you might encourage collaboration if learners can get together in **self-help groups**. Inexperienced learners can be very nervous to begin with, so working with a fellow-learner can help to boost confidence. Undertake **developmental testing** of both the procedures and your instructions for them so that you can be sure that all the suggested activities are unambiguous and safe, and that you get some idea of the varieties of avenues of exploration that can open up. Your learners may surprise you! (Be careful about safety legislation such as the UK Health and Safety at Work Act and check legal liability for accidents.)

Many of the aims of practical work can be achieved using some substitute experience. If *video* is available learners can follow experiments step-by-step, see the equipment set up, make notes on any visible or audible effects, take down the reading each time the camera zooms in on a measurement device, process the data they have gathered and then go on to check their conclusions. A well-presented substitute experience of this kind may be better than the real thing in some respects, since unlike most experiments, the video player can usually be stopped at will, wound forwards or backwards at speed and repeated several times if necessary. You can also use video to provide access to simulated real-life situations that, because of expense, danger or other impracticalities, could not normally be provided for learners at all.

You can achieve almost as much as you can with video, but with much less elaborate equipment, by using *audiovision*. This is a combination of audio cassette and visual material such as photographs, line drawings, microscope slides, flow charts, circuit diagrams, statistical or other tables, charts, maps, plaster casts, fossils or anything else that learners should observe closely and systematically with a guiding voice in their ears.

Various kinds of computer simulation can also be used to good effect and have the advantage of not being tied to real time or real life. Things that happen in a few microseconds can be slowed down infinitely, and a few million years of cosmological processes can be simulated in a few minutes.

preparatory material see *remedial material*.

prerequisites for a lesson/module/course are the knowledge, skills, relevant experience, and perhaps attitudes the teacher would like the learners to have before starting on some particular learning experience. In the planning stage, those skilled in *educational technology* or instructional design, among others, try to analyse and specify the indispensable prerequisites as closely as possible, and sometimes refer to them as the entry behaviour for the course. In reality, specifying the prerequisites in advance does not necessarily mean that every learner will have mastered them before starting the lesson or course. People have been known to pass the *pre-tests* that demonstrate their prerequisite knowledge, and to have forgotten it as soon as they begin the new piece of learning. Since learners are all different, and learning is not necessarily either linear or hierarchical, useful learning often takes place in the absence of a total mastery of the prerequisites.

All this does not mean that it is unnecessary or optional for the designer of self-instructional materials to attempt to describe the things that learners should know, or be able to do, before they begin their lesson or open their first learning package. All teaching has to start somewhere, and it is best when that somewhere is, at least approximately, where the average learner happens to be. A good face-to-face teacher may run a sort of educational community taxi service, as far as possible picking up each learner at their own individual starting point. When preparing self-instructional materials, however, it is more like organizing a bus service. Both teacher and learners need to know where the bus is going to, ie the *objectives*, but first of all they need to know where it is going to leave from, ie the prerequisites.

Whether or not all the learners actually choose to learn in the teacher's chosen sequence of study, it is often useful to assume that learning is a hierarchical process, in which topics D, E and F automatically follow topics A, B and C. If this is done, then it becomes clear that A, B and C are the prerequisites needed before D, E and F can be tackled. Gagné suggested that it is possible to work backwards from the main objectives to seek out a hierarchy of 'enabling objectives', by asking what learners must be able to do before they can achieve final mastery. In this way you could work back to what learners must know and be able to do before they begin work on your course. However, if you are preparing materials for a course that is well known to you, the chances are that decisions of this kind have already been taken and when you are designing lesson 4, the prerequisites will be lessons 1, 2 and 3. No matter how you arrive at them, it is important to know and be able to describe the prerequisites before you begin to plan the materials.

It is often specific skills rather than factual knowledge that can be seen to be important prerequisites. Your course may demand a certain level of algebraic manipulation or musical notation, and be incomprehensible to those who have not reached that level. In particular, subjects that are based upon special forms of notation or special languages call for precise specification of the skills that learners will need before they can begin to study.

Having specified your prerequisites, and informed your learners of them, you should stick to them without adding anything. Any new skills you find are necessary will have to be included in the teaching. It has been known for learners to be assured that nothing but simple arithmetical skill would be called for, and then, to their consternation, to be expected to be familiar with a number of statistical processes. This is nothing short of cheating by the teacher.

presentation (typography and format) The decisions that are made about the typography and format of written material can have important effects on its quality. Presentation can affect learners at a number of different levels from the convenience of the size and weight of the materials to the ease with which they can overview the text from its graphic appearance.

Format. The format of a text is the size and orientation of the page. The size is determined by three factors:

- The printing and binding systems to be used – cheaper systems prevent the use of large or non-standard paper sizes.
- The needs of the user – the text should be small and light if it is to be carried in pockets or handbags.
- The nature of the content – for example, it is easier to incorporate *illustrations* in the text if a relatively large format is used.

Inevitably, the actual size will often be a compromise between competing considerations, and may be standardized within an institution or organization.

Paper is supplied in standard sizes. Non-metric sizes are still used in the USA and by book publishers. In Europe the A series of international sizes predominates for business and educational stationery. The B and C series relate to posters and envelopes. The most popular A sizes are A4 (210 × 297 mm) and A5 (210 × 148 mm) so that A5 is exactly half the size of A4, with the same proportions. Similarly A6 is half A5 and so on.

Binding system. If your text is printed on office machinery that can print only single pages, you will find that most of the office binding systems waste about half an inch of the page width thus constraining your layout options. The cheapest system, stapling along the side, may prevent the text from staying open. Plastic-comb binding, or punched holes for the learner to use some form of loose-leaf binding, may be better. If your text is commercially printed, the binding should hold together satisfactorily and stay open flat on a table for study. The two main systems are saddle stitching – wire staples along the spine, and so-called 'perfect' binding – square-backed books glued along the spine.

Page layout. Unless you have the services of a professional graphic designer – or are very skilled with the desktop publishing software on your wordprocessor – it is best to stick to a single column layout. For this the two main considerations are margins and the width of the column of type. Generous margins are very useful where self-instructional materials are concerned: the binding system may require them, learners find them useful for making notes, and the writer can use them for side headings, 'flags', or study guidance notes. Much self-instructional material makes use of *icons*, such as a pencil, a book or audio-tape, to signal activities, reading from other material or a change of medium. The exact size of margins is related to the choice of column width, and this in turn depends to some extent on the choice of typeface. A width of between 8 and 12 words on average is desirable.

Choice of type. There are two main styles for continuous reading; roman and sanserif. Roman types have small cross-strokes ('serifs') at the end of each main stroke of the letter, the individual letters vary considerably in width, and the vertical strokes are thicker than the horizontal, as if drawn with a broad-nibbed pen. Sanserifs are more recent and systematic in design – they have no serifs and the letters are drawn with a more even stroke width.

The more traditional roman types are regarded as being more legible than sanserifs for long periods of continuous reading, although sanserifs are perfectly acceptable for shorter passages and are considerably clearer for the printing of tables. The two styles can be used in parallel – for example, roman type for the main text, and sanserif for exercises or study notes. Each typeface has an associated 'family' of italic and bold versions. These can be used for emphasis within the main text, and for signalling headings, summaries and other components. There are numerous decorative display types available for major headings and cover designs.

Some principles of good legibility:

- Most importantly, the horizontal emphasis of the line must not be disrupted. Problems can be presented, for example, by sanserif type which has a strong up-and-down vertical stress or by excessively wide spaces between words.
- Line length should not exceed an average of 12 words per line, ie 72 letters and spaces. For 'justified' type (with a straight right-hand edge) 8 words is the normal minimum; for unjustified type, a narrower column is acceptable. The reason for this is that the word spaces in very narrow justified columns sometimes have to be excessively wide, as you can see from any newspaper.
- For most readers, 10 or 11 point type is the most legible for continuous reading. This book has been set in 11 point type. The point is a traditional unit of measurement – there are 72 points to the inch. You may encounter 'pica', which is 12 points, while 7 or 8 point type may be used for tables, footnotes, and references, etc.

Typographic structure. In addition to ensuring the legibility if continuous prose, the typography of a piece of self-instructional material can play an important part in displaying the overall structure of its content. If adequately signalled, *headings*, *summaries* and other learning aids can make the text more accessible to a learner who is browsing, looking for an *overview*, doing *revision*, or looking for a particular piece of information (see *access devices*).

pre-tests are tests given to learners before they begin a lesson/module/course. They serve one or both of two main purposes:

- They check that the learner has the necessary prior knowledge, skills, and perhaps attitudes, ie the *prerequisites*.
- The results obtained in pre-tests can be compared with those obtained in the subsequent *post-tests* to establish how much the learner has learned. This may be important in *developmental testing*.

If you have specified your prerequisites adequately, it is relatively straight-forward to design a suitable pre-test that will establish that the learner has the appropriate *entry behaviour*. The process is similar to the devising of a post-test that exactly reflects the objectives of the learning experience.

How long should a pre-test be? The answer depends on what sort of learning experience it precedes. If it is the pre-test for a year long course, then it might be sensible to set a test that will take the learner an hour or more to complete. Alternatively, if it is a pre-test for a lesson that should take the learners about an hour, five minutes might be as much as you want them to devote to it, especially as distance learners will have to spend some time in checking the answers for themselves.

What if the required level is not attained? One thing you can do is to advise learners where to find the things that need brushing up. This at least gives the distance learner something positive to do. If you have the resources, you might prepare some *remedial* or *preparatory material* for learners who need it. If the learner is nowhere near the required level, you can only counsel them not to start the course and advise them on suitable preparatory courses.

projects The term 'project' is used when we require learners to conduct (usually for *assessment*) an independent piece of work, done either individually or in groups. Projects may take many forms: design projects, scientific experiments, survey research projects into social questions, information searches, etc. Experience shows that many types of project can be completed by distance learners working on their own, provided adequate time and guidance are available and that the resources, information or equipment likely to be needed are accessible to all learners.

Projects differ in the extent to which they are structured. A completely unstructured project is on a topic chosen by the learners who select and/or produce their own source material. In a completely structured project, learners work independently on a topic chosen by the teacher, who also selects the material on which the learners work – case studies for example. And there there are many degrees of structure in between. Very successful projects can be organized for distance learners where each individual collects a small amount of data, the data are pooled and then each individual can do different things with the resulting large database. Widespread geographical dispersion of distance learners can be used to advantage in projects, if learners contribute data to, say, a national survey of levels of particular pollutants or of genetic variations in plants or insects. Projects like this require very careful planning and organization but do give learners the satisfaction of participating in a major and worthwhile piece of work.

Learners who carry out well-designed projects have to deploy higher cognitive skills in organizing, analysing and synthesizing their material. They are encouraged to use their own initiative, to take responsibility for their own learning, and learn to apply theoretical knowledge to real problems. Most of them like project work and become very involved – sometimes too involved and the rest of their studies suffer! A few learners find the responsibility too much for them and need to change to something much more structured.

You need to allow quite a lot of time if your learners are to go beyond merely collecting information (see **workload**). It can be helpful to divide the project work into stages and allot a proportion of the total time to each stage, for example:

- Choosing the topic – 10 per cent
- Designing a plan of action – 10 per cent
- Collecting source material – 40 per cent
- Organizing the data – 20 per cent
- Presenting/reporting/evaluating the outcome – 20 per cent

It is easy to underestimate the time needed for this kind of work. Structured projects need a minimum of 25 hours, and unstructured ones, 50 hours. The average time spent by learners is likely to be double that. You can get a sensible idea of the time needed for your own kind of project by **developmental testing**. This will also give you guidance as to how much structuring is needed and how much information you need to supply in a ready-to-use form.

Learners should be graded on the processes they use to tackle the project rather the success or failure of the end product. Complete failures can result in more learning taking place than in many a (perhaps lucky) success.

There are three points at which **tutorial support** is particularly useful:

- In the initial selection of the topic; learners often need to be guided towards feasible, rather than exciting and ambitious, projects.
- In where to get the information, and what to do with it.
- In providing detailed help with processing and presentation.

This can be done at a distance by, say, requiring each learner to submit progress reports at stages, perhaps as formal **assignments**. **Telephone tutorials** are also of great value.

Q

quality control is a blanket term which covers all the processes that are intended to ensure that the product that goes to the consumers is as good as circumstances allow it to be. In practice, there may be a bracket of acceptability ranging from the lower limit of 'will do' to the upper limit of 'further improvement unnecessary'. It would be disappointing and unprofessional, however, if for economy reasons and time pressure, most self-instructional material fell into the 'just good enough' category; or indeed if we never tried to raise the upper limit. Quality control of self-instructional materials should be a permanent process. However modest the start level, experience with the initial product can lead to improved versions and better learner performance and satisfaction next time around.

If you are working on your own designing self-instructional materials and using them in your teaching, you will need to enlist help from other people to ensure the quality of your product. There are four points that are important for quality control.

1. Early draft. Show this to some trusted colleague(s) for comment and constructive criticism. The best of us make unsuspected mistakes that are immediately spotted by another pair of eyes, and several heads are often better than one when they pool their experience and expertise. Bear in mind that teaching through self-instructional materials is a more public activity than face-to-face teaching in a closed classroom. Colleagues, and many other people, will undoubtedly see your 'teaching', so enlist their support at this stage rather than receive their comments and opinions when they are too late to be useful.

2. Later draft. In practice, this may be a second, third or even fourth draft and should have been through ***developmental testing*** of some kind. A ***tutorial try-out*** is simplest, easiest to arrange, and usually very effective.

3. Handover draft. At this point ***editing*** is essential, preferably by someone other than the writer, before the draft is reproduced for use by learners.

4. Final product. This should be further developed (particularly in the early days) in the light of ***feedback*** gained from users during ***course presentation and monitoring***, so that the learners themselves are involved in quality control.

A fuller account of each individual process is given elsewhere under the appropriate heading. When materials are being designed by course teams there are usually planned points in the formal scheduling when these processes take place.

Such processes are particularly concerned with the teaching quality of the materials. Distance teaching institutions are also likely to have additional, built-in quality control mechanisms related to academic or professional credibility and any materials produced for them are likely to be subject to external academic assessment before being made available to learners.

Quality control is important in open and distance learning because at any one time the materials may be the only teaching that the learner gets. Your materials should therefore be able to stand on their own. This is quite obvious as far as *distance learners* are concerned, but even if you intend the materials for use in an open or flexible learning situation with considerable *tutorial support*, the materials should be good enough to enable the learner to make progress when no other help is immediately available. The particular advantage of self-instructional materials is that they enable learners to choose their own time and place of study. Poor quality materials cannot do this, and if learners come to a frustrated halt every time they try to study them, they become prime candidates for *drop-out*.

questions Well-designed self-instructional materials rely very heavily on a variety of types of questions that have been included for a number of different reasons. Rhetorical questions are used for their stylistic effect, and to let the learner pause and think briefly, but all other questions call for answers or *feedback*. Usually it is the learner who is called on to supply the answers, so that many questions are also in effect *activities*. Equally, many activities are phrased, or could be phrased, as questions.

In open and distance learning, questions can have a number of useful functions. They can help to keep learners alert, to assess their own progress, to highlight and reinforce what has been learnt, to link one piece of learning with another, and to provide ready access for study and *revision*. If the questions are asked as part of an *assignment* or any other piece of work submitted for *marking* and grading, they can provide a measure of the learners' performance for both learner and teacher. A distinction is sometimes drawn between 'teaching' questions and 'testing' questions or '*formative*' and '*summative*' questions, but these descriptions usually refer to the teacher's main motive in asking the questions rather than to the intrinsic nature of the questions themselves. Learners are likely to perceive any 'teaching' question as, to some extent, a test. They should also be learning something even when they are attempting a test that has ostensibly been set purely for the purpose of grading them.

Questions can vary considerably in length, or rather, the answers may take the learner varying lengths of time. Distance learners should always be given a clear indication of the approximate length of time that they should spend on each question (or question type). If you do not do this, you tend to add to the general climate of uncertainty that is one of the chief problems of distance learners, and those learners who find the question unexpectedly difficult, or especially stimulating, may spend hours on something for which you have (in your own mind) allowed only two or three minutes. It is up to you, as the teacher, to decide on the appropriate length of learner activity that the question is designed to stimulate and, in doing so, to give an indication of its relative importance. (See also *computer-marked assignments, in-text questions, post-test, pre-tests, self-assessment*.)

R

radio is sometimes an option for distance education systems. The *audio* component of learning materials can be broadcast using ground-based or satellite-based channels. Radio can serve many of the same purposes as audiotape although it is ephemeral unless learners have the capability of recording broadcasts. It has the advantage of being relatively inexpensive to create, is easy to change and update and is often the most current component of a learning package. It can be an important way of keeping in touch with learners and creating a sense of identity for a widely-spread learning community. If created just-in-time or even broadcast live it offers opportunities to respond to learners' questions and difficulties. With two-way links or in conjunction with the telephone it can be used as a tutorial medium and it can help to pace learners as it happens at fixed times.

radiovision is the use of visual material along with radio broadcasts as in *audiovision*. Its scope is more limited than audiovision because pace and time is dictated by the broadcast. Pausing long for thought, activity or repetition is not possible.

readability Will the target audience for our self-instructional materials find the materials readable? That is, not just engaging and interesting, but written in a *style* and at a level commensurate with their average reading ability. This is quite an important question, particularly if you know that you may be catering for people with fairly low reading ages or levels. Of course one of your main aims may be to increase learners' facility with the written word, but you will have to start where they are rather than where you want them to finish!

There are several ways of judging readability (and what follows is discussed in terms of the English language):

- *Depend on individual reader judgement* (your own?). This approach is not very reliable, for three reasons. Readers vary, according to their experience, in their competence to judge; English is an extraordinarily rich language, not easy to judge for readability; and much depends on how novel the subject-matter is to the readers.

- *Depend on group judgement.* If you ask five or six readers to judge readability, you get a better estimate, close to that obtained by the next two methods. In practical terms, however, it may be difficult and even expensive to arrange for group judgement but readability could be included in **developmental testing** questions.
- *Test learner comprehension.* If you use tests to find out which passages learners have understood best, that will give you some estimate of relative readability. The results may be confounded, however, by other factors such as learner ability, test conditions or other problems with your materials.
- *Use a readability test.* This will predict how difficult the learners are likely to find your material. It can usually be used easily on samples of what you write, long before learners read them, thus avoiding costly and embarrassing errors.

There are several tests of readability available, and some are not difficult to apply. (If you are working with a wordprocessor you may have a software package which will do it for you.) They all depend on some combination of word and sentence length. This is because as a general rule, longer words and longer sentences make for harder reading. If you use such a test, it will give you a rough indication of whether you need to use shorter words and sentences, ie simpler language.

Let us try the Gunning Fog Index to judge how foggy, or heavy, some writing can be. It is calculated like this. Find the average number of words per sentence in a typical passage of about 100 words. Then find the percentage of words with three or more syllables, excluding (a) capitalized ones, (b) words consisting of short easy ones, and (c) verbal forms made into three syllables by endings such as -ed and -ing. Add the two numbers together and multiply by 0.4 to get the index number. If it is above 12, you are in trouble, assuming you are teaching people who have left school.

If you apply the Fog Index to the last paragraph you should find the index number to be about 10.5. So overall it isn't foggy, although some parts are obviously less penetrable than others. Alternatively I could have written the same information this way:

Fog Index (FI) of a piece of writing, based on a sample of 100 words is:

FI = 2 (Average sentence length + percentage long words)

where
- average sentence length is number of words/number of sentences
- long words are those with three or more syllables.

But this mixes languages – English and mathematical notation – and will be less foggy to those fluent in mathematical language but incomprehensible to those who are not. This is another problem in judging readability.

There is an indicator which is even simpler to calculate. The Complexity Quotient is simply the average number of long words per sentence. Just take the number of complete sentences on a page and divide that by the number of long (three or more syllables) words on the page. A complexity quotient greater than three suggests that your prose is more difficult than that of many novelists or authors writing for non-specialists – or that you are writing in a subject area with its own complex, technical language.

These indices are just guides and the most important point to remember in using them is that they give pointers to making your writing clearer. If your score is high, try to lower it by breaking up sentences or using simpler words. Needless to say, you should avoid being mechanistic about this. Some of the greatest writers of fiction write in very long sentences, using complex and expressive language. For non-fiction and particularly for teaching through writing, we all need to watch out for fog.

The readability of your material does not only depend upon word and sentence length, it is also affected by the *style* in which you write. For teaching purposes, you should aim for maximum clarity. (See *access devices, advance organizers, headings, overviews, presentation*.)

reading speeds Apart from the readability of your printed material, you should also be concerned about its length. If your target audience includes some slowish readers, you will need to know roughly how long they are likely to take to read through your material even once, let alone study it closely.

It is difficult to give accurate estimates for average reading speeds for different audiences. Reading speeds vary considerably, depending on the type of material and the purpose in reading it. (Again, what follows refers to reading English.) People *scan* some texts very fast indeed (perhaps over 1,000 words per minute) to find something. They *skim* other texts almost as quickly (700 wpm) when they want to get a general idea of what is in them. A 'light novel' they may read at 250–300 wpm. Still other texts, like this one, they only read parts of, for reference, but they may read these quite slowly (200 wpm). Instructional texts on the whole require slow reading (80–100 wpm), with frequent reference back if readers are trying to master the content.

Mathematical texts are read extremely slowly (50 wpm), particularly if readers are expected to do a fair amount of problem-solving along the way.

As an easily remembered basis for a first rough estimate, learners can read:

Easy text	100 words per minute
Average text	70 words per minute
Difficult text	40 words per minute.

Assuming that you have to aim most of the time at average learners, you can find out how long it will take them as part of **developmental testing**. The figures you get will, if anything, underestimate the time needed. If you cannot carry out trials, at least you can count the number of words, take into account the type of material to be read, and use the figures above to estimate the time required. Nothing is so discouraging to learners using self-instructional materials than to be told they must read far more in a given time than they can possibly manage. They will react by skipping, not even skimming, large chunks of your carefully prepared material. (See also **workload**).

reflective action guide is a description, given by Rowntree (1992), of one of the two main teaching styles he identifies in self-instructional materials:

> The reflective action guide assumes that the important learning will take place away from the package. The material is a guide to action elsewhere – in real situations, perhaps with real people. The aim is not to have the learner master a body of knowledge but to attain personal insights or practice towards some kind of practical competence. . . .
>
> But the reflective action guide is not just a set of instructions. . . . It requires learners to think critically about the why and how of what they are doing and to evaluate the outcomes.
>
> The reflective action guide may have fewer activities than the tutorial-in-print but they will be more time consuming. The reader may spend far more time on the activities than on reading the text.
>
> Also, the activities are more likely to be related to the learner's own situation than to sample situations or case studies posed by the author. They are also less likely to involve writing or keying answers to questions about what the author has said in the package. On the contrary, they are likely to involve going out to do something away from the package.
>
> The learner may well be expected to interact with other people as part of an activity. The author cannot know enough about the learner's situation to provide specific feedback, so the learner must gather his or her own. (p.135)

(See also **tutorial-in-print**.)

reinforcement see *feedback*.

remedial material is additional material that is intended to help learners who, for any of a number of reasons, do not learn well enough or fast enough from the main materials. It can be of several types.

- Material intended to help learners reach the **prerequisites** before they begin a course, eg, a preparatory package for learners who need to brush up their mathematics before beginning a science course.
- Material to which learners can be referred during the course if they require further explanation or more practice, eg, an exploratory sheet explaining what is meant by 'critical path analysis' for learners who, in working through the main materials, have just met the term for the first time.
- Material which helps learners develop study skills appropriate to the sort of courses they are embarking on.

You do not necessarily have to provide extra materials at all points where some of your learners experience difficulty, and you do not necessarily have to write all the extra material yourself. Where the learning problem is concerned with a point that you have already explained elsewhere in the materials, it is often enough to give a page number (perhaps in a footnote) to learners who need help. If there is a suitable textbook available, or material for an earlier module or course, you can refer learners to the pages that provide both explanation and practice exercises.

The quantity and scope of any remedial material you write yourself will depend upon the resources that you can devote to it. As a limited provision, you might identify a few points that in your experience, or in that of those carrying out **developmental testing**, present difficulties to some learners, and write a 'help sheet' for each learning problem. At the other end of the scale, the ideal might be to write very full explanations that virtually amount to a complete parallel course for slow learners.

Remedial material, like any other form of learning material, can be delivered in a number of ways. If you are able to select the most flexible and responsive system, one common strategy is to use a limited face-to-face tutorial component for this purpose. Otherwise, perhaps a change of medium would be helpful. A more ambitious form of provision is to design interactive **computer-assisted** tutorials as an alternative to the explanations given in the main text. The self-pacing and immediate **feedback** provided in this way can make tutorials of this kind a particularly attractive form of remedial provision. Alternatively, using audiotape in some way to provide additional approaches can give a feeling of individual and personal support.

residential course/school is a chance for learners to come together for a short period of concentrated study. The time is usually used to mount learning experiences that are difficult to provide otherwise such as laboratory work, intensive computer work, role play, oral work in languages, field work, etc. In *work-based* open *learning*, residential courses can be seen as incentives or rewards. In distance learning, they are an opportunity to reduce isolation and allow learners extensive interaction with one another. Residential courses can be an expensive component of a learning package so your learners, especially if they are paying for their courses themselves, will need to be assured of the need for a residential course and of learning value for money.

resource-based learning occurs when individuals or small groups of people learn from such things as self-instructional materials, textbooks and apparatus or exhibits of various kinds. Open and distance learning may use any of these, and are thus, by definition, forms of resource-based learning. Not all resource-based learning systems are suitable for distance learning, though, because many of them require the presence of a tutor to carry out such tasks as organizing small groups, doing oral work or practical demonstrations, providing remedial tuition, supervising stage tests, etc. The resources for such learning systems are often kept in one location such as a library or resource centre and the learners come to that location to use the material. Resource-based learning is clearly an attractive idea to anyone who believes that learners should take an active part in their own learning and education. It is also, potentially at least, much less dependent on time and space constraints than more conventional forms of education. (See also *learning workshop*.)

revision as the term implies, refers to the activity of studying again materials already studied at least once (known as reviewing in the USA).

Even at a distance you can do various things to help your learners to revise. For example, the *activities* and *in-text questions* that are embedded at suitable places in the text can be used by learners who wish to review the material. Other *access devices* (eg, contents page and index) will help your learners to search the text quickly and cross-reference the concepts in it. A set of learning *objectives*, placed at the beginning or end of the text as appropriate, is a useful checklist for learners who want to revise the material.

Of course it tends to be the imminence of *examinations* that stimulates the revision process. If you have a limited amount of face-to-face tuition available, some support in preparation for examinations is always appreciated. A sample examination paper or two, with specimen answers, will certainly help your learners to know what to expect. You can tell them what proportion of their time they should try to allow for revision. You should already have given them some idea of the relative importance of each part of their course and clear indications of any options they have about routes through the material. Bear in mind that uncertainty is a real problem for distance learners and that they may have no one else to talk to, so tell them as much as you can without, of course, jeopardizing the security of the examination.

S

self-assessment in the education and training sense is a process in which we ask learners to answer *questions*, or carry out prescribed *activities*, and supply them with certain criteria against which to judge themselves. When we have asked a self-assessment question (often referred to as an SAQ), for example, we can supply either a 'correct' answer, or a discussion of possible answers. For more elaborate exercises or activities, we can provide learners with model answers, specimen answers or our own response to the activity so that they can compare their own efforts.

Self-assessment is a purely voluntary thing and learners often need to be convinced that it is very much in their own interests. It is not always sufficient to ask them well-framed questions and supply informative answers. You also have to make it clear where the self-assessment fits into their studies as a whole. Sometimes, of course, this may be clear enough; at others you may have to indicate how each activity contributes towards the *aims* and *objectives* of the course or lesson. In the self-instructional situation of course, there is no real alternative to the provision of a significant amount of self-assessment material. Even where there is *continuous assessment*, several constraints – time, money, and educational effectiveness – place limits on the number of marked and graded *assignments* that can be demanded of learners, who are thus forced to become their own assessors for most of the time.

There are many forms of self-assessment and you will find more about them under the headings: *activities, in-text questions, objective tests, post-test, pre-tests, questions* and *student-stoppers.*

self-help groups are formed when a number of learners (who might not otherwise meet) regularly contact each other to discuss their studies. By using self-instructional materials, and studying as individuals, open and distance learners (although enjoying many advantages) may be cut off from much of the support that students in a conventional situation get from their personal contacts with fellow-learners. This support takes many forms: emotional support in the form of sympathy to a fellow sufferer, say, or group support such as presenting a solid front against grievances. Learners also support one another educationally. They share their study problems with one another, try to reduce uncertainty by deciding on an agreed interpretation of teaching points that have not been clearly expressed and, very sensibly, discuss suitable approaches to *assignments* or other pieces of work that have to be submitted for *marking*.

If your learners are operating individually, but live reasonably near to each other or work in the same organization, it could have considerable benefits if you put them in touch with each other and suggest they form a self-help group. This is a voluntary activity so that how often and how formally they meet (if at all), and what they talk about will be for them to decide. It is not absolutely necessary that they meet regularly face-to-face, because many of the contacts can be by telephone and, by using a cheap amplifier, can even involve more than two learners at a time. (See *telephone tutorials*.) *Computer conferencing* might in some circumstances be an appropriate means of communication for a self-help group.

sequence and structure Since self-instructional material is basically written material, it is presented to learners with an effectively linear structure and most learners will probably study it that way unless otherwise instructed. However, there are a considerable number of possible sequences in which subject matter can be organized, some of which make study easier than others, and we need to devote some thought to the matter. We need to avoid illogical or erratic sequences in which the learner is continually being referred forwards or backwards to other parts of the material. We also need to consider providing alternative paths through the material; different learners may find different sequences helpful.

In many subjects there are sequences that provide a neat, and perhaps logical development of the topic. In electricity, for example, current, charge, potential, potential difference, Ohm's law, resistance, power, is the usual logical development in most physics textbooks. Many people might get lost, though, if they plough through this on their own. A classroom teacher would prepare the ground with some introduction and demonstrations or experiments, indicating the general direction to be followed. An alternative sequence that might work well with some people would be to start with Ohm's law, taking voltmeters and ammeters for granted, and then gradually refine the concepts. There is no absolutely best way. We have to try and find what is best for a particular *target audience*, given the purpose of their study. What is appropriate for budding research physicists may be quite irrelevant for trainee motor mechanics, but both need to understand Ohm's law.

Two common approaches to sequencing are 'bottom up' and 'top down'. Learners who favour the first approach prefer to master each topic in turn, and take it on trust that they will eventually be able to integrate them into a meaningful whole. Those who favour the second, prefer to get a view of the whole as quickly as possible, taking intermediate steps for granted, and go back to tackle each detail when they can see its relevance to the whole.

The basic sequence you have decided on may be modified into a sandwich structure for each main topic – introduction or **advance organizer** to set the scene, exposition, and **summary** or recapitulation. This basic structure can be repeated for each main topic or the topics can be nested within an overall introduction and summary. A further elaboration is the 'spiral' approach, in which each topic is taken up a number of times, being developed a little further each time.

Another approach to structuring the material, which caters for individual learner differences, is to use a branching structure that may use **pre-tests** and **post-tests** at appropriate points to route learners according to the present state of their knowledge. The various branches need not converge on the same end-point. In particular, towards the end of a course (or section), learners might be offered a choice of topics according to their interests or abilities. At intermediate stages, faster learners might be offered additional non-essential **enrichment** options.

A third basic structure that provides more scope for learner autonomy is that of 'mainstream and tributaries'. The mainstream covers the principle topics covered in the course, and the tributaries develop the skills and ancillary knowledge that the student must acquire in order to master the mainstream. For example, the mainstream might be concerned with National Insurance benefits, and the tributaries with statistics, Acts of Parliament, and calculation of benefit. The advantage of this is that learners can decide their own study sequence. Pre-tests may be built in at all the junctions to help learners decide whether they need to study the next tributary or not.

Some combination of these should meet most requirements. Whichever structure you adopt, it is essential to make clear to the learners what you are doing, what choices they have, what they are supposed to know, and what they can gloss over for the time being. It is also desirable to provide indications of shortcuts and bypasses to enable learners who get behind, in courses with fixed end-points, to omit the least essential parts.

signposting see *access devices*.

staff development/training is a collective term for the help given to people in an organization to improve their knowledge and skills and to develop in new directions. Opportunities can be presented formally through courses and workshops, either in-house or provided elsewhere, through open learning packages or with the guidance of a mentor. Informally, people learn on the job, from one another, through mentoring or through peer-group reflection. Preparing open and distance learning materials as part of a team can be a considerable developmental process for everyone involved.

In the context of open and distance learning, people often have to adapt existing professional skills, develop new ones and possibly change attitudes. Some people will need the opportunity to explore the potential of open and distance learning in order to be convinced that it is a sound and viable approach to the education and training they are charged with providing. People accustomed to face-to-face teaching may need to develop writing skills, others may need to learn about print or media production or about the management of large-scale learning systems. Support staff, tutors and those offering **counselling**, will need to explore differences that openness and distance bring to their roles and will need to practise such skills as giving **feedback** on **assignments**, holding **telephone tutorials** and managing **computer conferencing**.

student-stoppers Whenever we include any **self-assessment** items in our self-instructional materials, we have to supply the 'correct' answers or, in some other way, suggest criteria by which learners may assess their own responses. Student-stoppers are devices to remind learners that it is time to stop and think before going on to the next section, which will usually include the answer(s). Student-stoppers can be used in **audio** and **video** materials as well as written ones; here is an example of a typical written one:

Q. What might a typical student-stopper look like?

****

A. Like the row of asterisks above.

You could equally well warn the learner by 'centring' the question:

Q. Is this in the middle?

or by having some other device to signal questions and their answers:

☐ What two factors can you think of which may be responsible for the extinction of a species?
■ Loss of the place where species live (their habitat) or direct reduction of their numbers by hunting.

Whichever form of student-stopper you decide to use, it is advisable to keep to the same form throughout, so that your learners will immediately know what to do whenever they come across one.

If we assume that most learners are willing to accept our advice and make at least some attempt at self-assessment items, the function of the student-stopper is, first of all, to remind them that here is some kind of *question* or *activity* that calls for a response before they go on and, secondly, to help them avoid learning the answer(s) inadvertently and prematurely. Although separated from the question by a student-stopper, the answer(s) should still be readily available when the learners need them. If you relegate them all to the very end of the materials, print them upside down, or on separate sheets (as is sometimes done), you run the risk of making them much less accessible for the learner. If questions and answers are too far apart, moreover, they are less useful as *access devices* for *revision*.

Sometimes the answers do need to be 'hidden' and occasionally, where the answer to a technical question, for example, is a graph or diagram of a distinctive shape, it is best to arrange for learners to have to turn the page in order to see it. Otherwise, even though they are interrupted by the student-stopper, the recognizable shape (which is the answer) may be perceived at the fringe of their vision.

There is no guarantee, of course, that a student-stopper will make learners stop and think. As far as *in-text questions* are concerned, some people find they learn best by reading the answer at once, without trying to discover it for themselves, and only then trying to analyse just why it is the 'correct' answer. Some people read the whole text through quickly the first time, answers and all, and only attempt the questions at the second more deliberate reading. It is all a matter of *learning style*.

Student-stoppers in audio and video materials serve exactly the same purpose. A standard tone, or snatch of music, for example, can warn learners to switch off the cassette player and turn it back on when they have completed the activity that has just been suggested.

study guide is a term that is applied to anything which gives guidance to the learner, from some notes on how to read a particular book (see *wraparound*) to a user's guide to a complete learning package (see *course guide*.) Sometimes a writer will put a short study guide at the beginning of each section of a large package or course to highlight the *aims* and *objectives* of that particular section and to draw attention to the introduction of new teaching techniques or media and any extensive or novel activities that the learner will be expected to undertake. Another current use of the term is to describe an extensive piece of material which effectively contains all the self-instructional elements of a package or course and which accompanies a book, collection of readings or other resource material. This is essentially the same as wraparound except that here the writer is likely to have produced the resource material as well but for some reason, possibly to do with production or publication, has chosen not to integrate the teaching physically with the other material.

study time see *workload*.

style is the general impression made by the way in which we select and shape our communications with our learners. It is distinct from content and teaching strategy, but it influences and is influenced by them. Style affects the overall tone of our approach to our learners and the kind of relationship or 'social climate' that we set up. In face-to-face teaching, our informal interactions with people and our non-verbal cues are an important part of our overall style. In self-instructional materials, our choice of words, sentence structure and presentation, make up much of our style. What should your style be? Like that of a textbook? A scholarly paper? A lecture? An individual tutorial?

Probably the best style to develop is a conversational one, like an individual tutorial. Textbooks try to be complete and authoritative but are usually designed to go along with face-to-face teaching and require some guidance for individual study. Scholarly papers are written to impress critical colleagues who, unlike learners, are already well-acquainted with the subject; it could be very off-putting to address learners in this way. A good lecture is pitched at the right level for learners, but contains many non-verbal cues that cannot easily be put down on paper. Also, it is usually only at the end, if at all, that there is any opportunity for question and answer. In all these three models it is the teacher who is doing almost all the work. In an individual tutorial, on the other hand, a good tutor will make sure that the learner is kept permanently active by being asked questions, invited to suggest examples, called upon to express opinions and then justify them, etc.

In an individual tutorial, of course, teacher and learner are in the same room, whereas you may never meet the learners who are going to work from your materials. Nevertheless, by using *activities*, *self-assessment*, *in-text questions*, etc, you can give learners plenty of opportunity for interaction with the material. How, though, can you supply the relatively informal, personal and supportive atmosphere of a good tutorial? It has to come through your writing style. It should sound as though it is addressed personally to one reader, it should be conversational in tone, and should relate to the sort of experience that you would expect the typical learner to have. It should aim at readability, keeping to short words and short sentences as far as possible. Address the reader as 'you' and do not be afraid to be present in your writing and call yourself 'I'. There are also times when it is useful to use 'we' as a kind of compliment to imply that you and the learner are members of the same special group. (See also *tutorial-in-print* and *reflective action guide*.)

summaries Just as an *overview* at the beginning of a lesson or course gives learners a holistic picture of what they will be asked to do, so a summary at the end of a section or a final summary should present a synthesis of what has been done and, hopefully, learned. This is because teaching, more often than not, consists of presenting the appropriate subject matter in small manageable parts. The judicious selection and presentation of these small parts, one at a time, is one of the professional skills of the teacher. So is their reassembly into a meaningful whole. Synthesis is a skill you may wish your learners to acquire, in which case asking them to write their own summaries every so often is a useful *activity*. Many common features of self-instructional materials are, in one way or another, summaries of the larger component of which they are a part. *Aims* and *objectives* summarize in their own particular way the learning materials to which they refer. *Pre-tests* and *post-tests* are summaries (because only rarely can you test everything) of what the learner should be able to do before and after the course. *Course guides* summarize, and offer advice on, whole courses. All summaries, no matter what their primary function, are also *access devices*, and should be structured so that they can be used by learners for *revision*.

summative is a word that is often used in the terms 'summative *evaluation*' and 'summative *assessment*'. Summative evaluation consists of investigating institutions, courses, materials, etc, in order to make some kind of formal judgement about them, eg, that they can be declared successful, or that they are academically acceptable, or perhaps that they should be abolished. Summative assessment consists of making rather similar judgements about learners and often produces stark pass-or-fail results. An end-of-course *examination* is one typical piece of summative assessment.

summer school see *residential school*.

support in open and distance learning systems usually refers to the help learners receive in addition to the learning materials. It comes in many forms and may be organized or informal, provided by tutors, counsellors, trainers, line managers, colleagues, other learners and families. It can be made available by a variety of means including face-to-face, post, telephone and electronic. (See *computer-mediated communication, counselling, marking, self-help groups, telephone tutorials, tutorial support*.)

supported self-study is the term used more frequently in schools for open or flexible learning. It places particular emphasis on the need for support from tutorials and the importance of the learner becoming actively involved in the learning process.

T

target audience is the group of learners for whom materials, courses or learning opportunities are being designed. Defining the target audience is an important part of the process of designing open and distance learning systems and materials. You will need to know something about the learner characteristics, what these people are hoping to learn and why, and how many of them there are likely to be over what period of time. (See *learner characteristics, learner profile*.)

teaching order see *sequence and structure*.

teleconferencing A system of linking individual telephones into a common network so that a group conversation can ensue. Very useful for *telephone tutorials*.

telephone tutorials are a useful means of supporting people's learning when distance or other constraints, such as travel costs or being homebound, make face-to-face meeting impossible. Tutoring by telephone offers an immediate and interactive form of contact that can help to reduce the sense of isolation experienced by remote learners, and can help motivate learners to persist with their studies. It also enables the learner with a particular problem or query to get quick *feedback* from a tutor or course writer or, where group tutorials are organized by telephone, to join in discussion with fellow learners.

Telephone tutorials can be organized in different ways depending on the role you want them to fulfil in your teaching scheme and the financial and technical resources you have available. Three possibilities using an ordinary public telephone system are:

- **One-to-one telephone tutorial**. Very like an ordinary telephone call, the learner and tutor discuss particular learning problems such as:

    . . . in Question 2, I don't understand this bit about the square root of -1, and I can't get any further with my next assignment . . . .

In this kind of tutorial no special equipment is needed other than a domestic telephone, and the costs are the same as for other calls.

- **Small group conference call.** This joins up to nine people, all at home using domestic telephones, into a common network. The call is booked in advance with the telephone company who link the individual lines by means of a conference combining unit, or 'bridge'.
- **Group tutorial using a loudspeaking telephone.** This is a relatively cheap amplifying device that enables a group of learners to sit round it at a study centre of some kind and talk to a remote tutor, using only one telephone line.

Telephone tutorials can be used effectively for tasks involving information transmission and exchange, problem-solving, and generating ideas. They are used in distance learning, often in conjunction with previously circulated materials, for planning *assignment* work, discussing short case studies, exchanging interpretations of a case or thesis, clarifying learners' difficulties with course material, manipulating symbolic expressions, interpreting sets of raw data, constructing and interpreting graphs, etc.

You may need to compensate for the lack of visual and graphic facility by the advance circulation of well-structured diagrammatic materials for use during the tutorial. These could include blank *diagrams* for completion, transparent overlays to build up a complex diagram, and the use of coloured sheets and reference grids for the easy identification of items.

Some adaptation is needed to become a telephone tutor. First, you need to be able to communicate, without being able to use *non-verbal cues*. Tutors holding group tutorials by telephone experience high initial anxiety, but quickly adapt to translating visual clues into verbal ones, signalling, for example, whose turn it is to speak or indicating an opening for a question. Telephone tutorials are more task-centred and more formal than a face-to-face meeting, and part of the tutor's work initially is to make the event more friendly and relaxed. Second, you may have to change your teaching strategy to suit the medium. Materials need to be more structured, more specific and circulated well in advance of the tutorial to allow sufficient preparation time by learners.

television Broadcast television programmes are sometimes an option for distance education systems, using national or educational television networks or satellite transmission. Television broadcasts can serve many of the same purposes as *video* although they are ephemeral unless learners have the capability of recording the broadcasts. Television is an expensive medium to work in and you need to be sure that the cognitive gain will be worth the expenditure. For effective learning from television you will probably need to provide support in the form of printed material, broadcast notes which suggest preparatory work, things to do while watching the broadcast and *activities* to follow up.

transformer is the term applied to a skilled communicator who 'transforms' material which is satisfactory from the point of view of the subject matter, but is inappropriately, or inadequately expressed. In open and distance learning, the 'skilled communicator' is most likely to be someone who is experienced in the design of self-instructional packages. The raw material which is inadequately or inappropriately expressed may be of two different types:

- Material that is perfectly good in its own way, but which has been produced for a different target population or for purposes other than self-instruction, eg, an article in a technical journal, or material that was originally designed for use in class-teaching.
- Material that is supposed to be self-instructional, but which has been produced by someone lacking the necessary skills.

Transformers are not normally experts in the subject matter concerned but they must be able to understand the material that has to be transformed. The necessary combination of self-instructional expertise and minimum subject competency may not be easy to find where the materials concerned are at a high level and/or highly technical in nature.

What detailed operations are included in 'transforming'? They can fall into any or all of the following categories:

- Considering the *aims* and *objectives* of the material, and spelling them out if they are clear but implicit. If not, then they have to be clarified with the original author or with other subject experts. Strictly speaking it would be overstepping the boundaries of transforming for transformers themselves to decide what the aims and objectives ought to be. It is of course essential that the aims and objectives are compatible with the rest of the package and/or course.
- Checking the *workload* to which the length of the material has to conform, and keeping this in mind throughout.
- Deriving, designing and adding where necessary, other characteristic features of self-instructional materials – *prerequisites*, *overviews*, cross-referencing, and a range of *activities*, *questions* and tests. These would normally include *pre-tests*, *in-text questions*, *post-tests* and provision for *self-assessment*.

- Checking that all these match the aims and objectives that were originally arrived at, adjusting the material (and aims/objectives too if it seems advisable), and repeating all this if necessary.

All of the above, of course, refers to written materials. If other media are involved, the transformer usually has two options:

- To make use of the existing *audio* or *video* components, using a study guide or commentary if necessary, to make sure that they are compatible with the rest of the course after it has been transformed.
- To re-specify, and remake the media components – a strategy which clearly calls for both time and money.

tutorial-in-print is a description, given by Rowntree (1992), of one of the two main teaching styles he identifies in self-instructional materials:

> The tutorial-in-print style is quite common among open learning workbooks and CBT packages. Learning from a tutorial-in-print is like having a good human coach or tutor, working with you one-to-one.
>
> Like a good human tutor, the package tells the learner what they are supposed to get out of the session and then explains the subject clearly with examples that tie in to their experience. However, unlike a lecturer (but like a one-to-one tutor), the package does not present a mono-logue. Instead, like a tutor, it asks the learner frequent questions to check that they have understood the ideas being discussed and can comment on them or use them.
>
> The tutorial-in-print style is perhaps most appropriate when there is a 'body of knowledge' to be mastered. Here the aim is to help the learner take on board a new way of looking at things. The writer sets frequent activities to ensure learners are keeping up with the argument. These activities focus on ideas and usually involve writing something down or tapping computer keys. The writer is able to give quite specific feedback because he or she knows the kind of thing that learners will have written. The learning is assumed to happen while the learner is interacting with the package. (p.134)

(See also *reflective action guide*.)

tutorial support Many open and distance learning systems include a certain amount of face-to-face contact with tutors, although this teaching element is obviously small compared with the role of the materials. The tutor is most likely to be a teacher who has not prepared any of the materials. It is easier, and in many ways better, when the face-to-face teaching is done by the authors of the materials but usually it is necessary to have the materials mediated by other tutors and they must be supported in order to contribute successfully to the system.

If you are planning a system which involves tutors, there are some questions to ask:

- What tutors are available?
- What do you want them to do?
- What should they actually teach in the face-to-face sessions?
- What should the tutor's defined role be?
- How can you help them to do it?
- How can you evaluate and improve the system?

What tutors are available? If your learners are individuals who are scattered geographically, you will probably have to select suitable centres at which learner numbers can be high enough to warrant looking for suitable locally-based tutors who could contribute on a part-time basis to your courses. Local colleges, firms or training organizations may form ready-made study centres that probably have suitable tutors available for you to recruit. (We are not here discussing the use of your materials by other autonomous organizations who would be responsible for developing their own tutorial support.) If you are running a high-level course with a relatively small group of learners, it may be best to have a tutor (yourself?) who travels to the learners. Despite all the travel that is involved, this may sometimes be both educationally effective and cost-effective; at least one Australian institution, for example, flies tutors to the outback.

What do you want them to do? Although you are using tutors to provide face-to-face tuition, probably their first and most important responsibility should be the **marking** of any coursework or **tutor-marked assignments** submitted by their group of learners. The provision to learners of suitable written *feedback* on their work is a valuable form of distance teaching, and it is desirable that this should be done by the person who from time to time meets the learners face-to-face. If some of your learners are likely to need **counselling**, an element of this could also be included in their responsibilities.

What should they actually teach in the face-to-face sessions? You can allow for various degrees of flexibility, from complete freedom to teach whatever they think best, to a defined role that is closely integrated with the materials. Complete freedom has its attractions but it can also present formidable problems. Some tutors may adopt a remedial approach, while others provide enrichment. There may be some who disagree so fundamentally with your whole approach that they confuse the learners by following an alternative programme of their own invention. If you wish your learners to enjoy a coherent set of learning experiences, you will probably wish to allocate a defined role to your tutors.

What should the tutors' defined role be? The systems approach to this problem is to treat the face-to-face sessions as one of the media through which your teaching will reach the learners. This means that, as with other media, you have to consider the characteristics of live tutors and make their role the subject of a suitable *media choice*. Your choice is clear enough if there are some parts of the learner's laboratory work, *practical work* or oral work that only a live tutor can do. Tutors are responsive, adaptive and good at supplying immediate feedback.They should always be asked to do those things which they can do and the materials cannot. One very common solution is to tie the tutors' role closely to *continuous assessment*, so that they spend most of their time on remedial work based on common errors in the last assignment, or helping learners to prepare for the next.

How can you help them to do it? If you decide to define the tutors' role fairly closely, it is only fair to give them detailed instructions. These are particularly important if they are distant tutors, ie, someone you may never see. They need not only to be familiar with the course materials but to be given a thoroughly professional briefing over and above anything that the learner receives. The briefing should, in the first place, deal with their approach to the course as a whole. Thereafter they should be given tutor's notes for each tutorial session. They will also need to be thoroughly briefed, and given practice, on their role as markers of assignments.

How can you evaluate and improve the system? By getting tutors to evaluate and improve themselves, because your tutorial support can only be as good as the tutors who provide it. Ideal tutors see themselves as an important and integral part of a team. Someone (you perhaps?) should be given responsibility for the occasional visit to, and discussion with the tutors for your course. Such meetings are never one-sided. Since your tutors are likely to be professional teachers or trainers in their own right, they can provide you with much valuable feedback about the effectiveness of the materials, the problems experienced by learners, and their own perceptions of their role. At the same time you can check that tutorial sessions are proceeding satisfactorily and keep an eye on such things as the maintenance of uniform marking standards in the tutorial body as a whole.

If the position is that you have supplied the materials, but that the local tutorial support is controlled by others, all you can do is to make certain that your tutor's notes are clear and complete and emphasize that any live teaching is to be considered an integral and far from unimportant part of the system. If your materials are of high quality they will be improved by good tutorial support and well able to withstand anything that is less than good.

In summary: get the best tutors you can, tell them exactly what you would like them to do, help them to do it and monitor them in a constructive way so that both you and they can improve your service to the learners.

tutorial try-out is a cheap and relatively easily organized way of using a very small number of 'guinea-pig' learners to make sure that draft materials are roughly on the right lines and contain no gross errors. It is a form of *developmental testing* that can be used on its own or as a preliminary to more ambitious forms such as field trials.

For a tutorial try-out you will need the services of four or five learners, similar to those for whom the material is intended but in the last resort any surrogate learners are better than none. Too large a group makes it difficult to discuss and observe at the same time. Trying out your materials with a group of learners in a tutorial setting can indicate any major difficulties in your material; you can test all the same things as you would in developmental testing. It also gives you an opportunity of discussing different approaches with learners while the difficulties are still fresh in their minds.

tutor-marked assignments (TMAs) These are pieces of coursework that learners submit for *marking*. In an open learning system where learners have contact with tutors or in a distance learning system which includes some face-to-face tutorial support, the best arrangement is when learners have their assignments marked by the same person who occasionally meets them. The marking of an assignment is an extremely important individual teaching and learning opportunity, often the only really interactive opportunity that a distance learner has. A tutor's *feedback* must be clear, supportive and as comprehensive as possible. Colleagues who tutor courses based on your material will need guidance and training in order to make the most of such teaching-by-correspondence.

typography see *presentation*.

V

validation of education or training is some test of whether a course or programme has succeeded in teaching what it set out to teach and whether this was a realistic educational or training need. Courses, including self-instructional ones, are validated in several ways: through well-qualified people being chosen to prepare or teach them; through expert assessors being appointed to inspect the course while under development; through obtaining *feedback* from learners and others once the course are being taught; and through experts sitting on *examination* or award boards that set the questions and decide the pass standard. All of these can help you validate your own self-instructional courses. Qualifications and institutions are validated in much the same ways. The opinions of acknowledged experts are vital in the process, but employers and the general public have influence too.

video Video material for education and training is generally speaking of two kinds.

- **Ready made** – material which has either been obtained from a commercial source (purchase, rent or occasionally free loan) or has been recorded (remember that there are *copyright* restrictions) from a televised or satellite broadcast. This sort of video is often of a standard length (eg, a 25-minute 'slot'), is designed to stand on its own to be comprehensible to a wide range of viewers, and is usually intended to be viewed from beginning to end, making no attempt to exploit the stop-start-replay facility of video cassette players. It is not primarily self-instructional material, although if suitable guidance is provided it might well form one component of a self-instructional package, always provided that the learner has access to a video player.
- **Purpose-made** – material which has been designed from the start to allow interaction with the learner. It is more likely to use the full potential of video-replay technology, such as the possibility of stopping, restarting, winding back, etc, to allow the learner to carry out various activities and perhaps to consult other pieces of material. If the learner

has ready access to a video player, this sort of material can be highly suitable for self-instruction.

The biggest constraint in using video as part of your self-instructional material is the need for each learner to have ready access to replay facilities. Of course many people do own video recorders but to assume that all learners will provide their own facilities can add a considerable extra cost to any course you might offer and could make study impossible for some people. Of course you could make replay facilities available at a study centre, learning workshop, workplace training centre or resource centre and make arrangements for learners to have access to these facilities by means of an appointments system. Someone must then be responsible for ensuring monitoring and maintenance of equipment because a single technical fault can lead to considerable frustration and a backlog of appointments. The use of centralized hardware also imposes an undeniable constraint on one of the most important advantages of self-instruction – learners being able to choose their own time and place of study. In this situation you have to weigh up the advantages of using video against the disadvantages of the delivery system. Unless its contribution to the package is unique and essential, the actual quality of the video component may be the determining factor.

The same problems come up in an even more severe form if you plan to dispense with all printed material and deliver your written messages, as well as your graphic ones, on the video screen. It is true that a video cassette (better still, a videodisc) can store a great many 'printed' pages, but if you decide to deliver your material to learners this way, you could liberate them from formal teaching, the fixed timetable and the classroom, only to chain them to the video screen. Printed material remains cheap, outstandingly portable, and almost infinitely repeatable. Furthermore, it is easier to find the place you want and the only hardware you need to make notes, alterations and additions to it is a pencil.

You may have video production facilities, including producers, at your disposal or may commission a production company. You may want or need to make your own. If you do there are three important principles to bear in mind:

- Learners must be able to follow both your presentation and any instructions associated with it – to switch off and carry out an activity, for example. Keep it simple.
- Learners must be able to see properly. No matter how simple your equipment, your choice of background, lighting and camera work are quite crucial.

- Learners must be able to hear properly. This means very careful planning if you have only one or two microphones.

What sort of things does video do well? You might want to use it for any of the following:

- To demonstrate practical work, tools, skills, and the correct use of equipment which, for reasons of accessibility or expense, cannot be done 'hands-on'.
- To illustrate motion and dynamic processes, eg, an aircraft in a spin.
- To model abstract (eg, mathematical) principles and processes.
- To demonstrate processes vividly through special devices such as animation, split-screen, slow motion, and speeded-up motion, eg, time-lapse photography for the germination of a seed.
- To take learners to places that would otherwise be inaccessible to them, eg, distant industrial plants or geological field trips.
- To demonstrate the relationship between different parts of a system, eg, between public transport provision and use of private cars.
- To provide (and sometimes to simulate) case-study material of actual events or human behaviour, eg, social interactions in a specific situation such as a classroom or a football crowd.
- To demonstrate faults and fault-finding procedures, eg, the effect of intermittent insulation breakdown in an ignition coil.
- To present anything that simultaneously requires sight and sound together with text and graphics, eg, the decoding, identification, and navigational use of information from radio beacons.
- To present a wide variety of resources in rich detail for learners to view as many times as they wish and to analyse and interpret at their own pace, so as to find out as much as possible for themselves.

vocational qualification is a statement of *competence* relevant to an occupation. (See *National Vocational Qualifications*.)

W

work-based learning is usually defined as some system which links learning to the work role. It is *learner-centred* and promotes the integration of structured learning in the workplace, provision of appropriate on-the-job training or learning opportunities and the identification and provision of relevant off-the-job learning opportunities. The purpose of work-based learning is to support workers and employers in their response to labour markets in which change has become endemic and to provide a basis for the provision of continuous learning opportunities which such change implies. By linking learning to the work role, motivation of both the employer and employee to support such learning is encouraged. It is not a specification of learning methods but it is obvious that there is a considerable role for open and flexible learning systems here.

workbook is somewhat similar to a *study guide* or *wrap-around* in that it usually contains the teaching elements, activities and guidance of the learning package. It also usually contains space and answer grids, etc for learners to keep records of what they do – for learners to work in. In some open learning systems learners are given the entire pack of materials. In others, such as learning workshops or work-based training systems where there is a high turnover of trainees, learners have access to all the materials but only own the workbook. This is a fairly economical way of providing learning materials but at the same time ensuring that learners have some record of what they have studied and a *revision* aid.

workload Unless we are very careful, self-instructional material can take far longer to study than was ever anticipated, leaving the learner with a tough choice between working excessive hours or not completing the work. Just occasionally the opposite also happens. Both these eventualities can be avoided if we are careful about the workload in our materials.

The first step is to determine the amount of work required in a course or package by, say, comparison with an equivalent face-to-face course. You will need to look at the content covered and the number of skills developed and the average time learners spend in formal teaching, practical work and private study. This will give an indication of how much time you can reasonably expect a learner to spend on the course or package and the content should be planned accordingly. Because teaching through self-instructional material is much more public than teaching in a closed classroom, there is often a temptation to write something that will be seen to be complete and definitive and that is, inevitably, grossly overloaded as far as the learners are concerned.

Estimating study time for materials is far from being an exact science but there are some rules of thumb and, with experience, you can make fairly accurate judgements. *Developmental testing*, of course, will give you some genuine estimates. The most basic thing to look at is how long the material will take to read. Although *reading speeds* vary from person to person, you can assume that the average is something like 100 words per minute for straightforward text. Learners might achieve twice this if you suggest they 'skim' read. On the other hand, for mathematical and closely argued text, the speed may drop to 50 words a minute or less. You need to allow time for re-reading all but the simplest passages – say an additional 50 per cent – and if learners are expected to commit things to memory, still more time is needed. Then you must add in time for *questions* and *activities*. If you have given suggested timings for activities in the materials you can work this out. But estimating those timings is not easy. Try writing what you would con- sider to be an adequate response to an activity; you may be surprised how long it takes you even when you have all the information at your fingertips. Learners are likely to take several times as long as you do to search out the information, think out what to say and write it.

The time it takes for learners to solve mathematical problems is even more difficult to judge; even the simplest may take up to 15 minutes or more. Learners may spend two or three hours struggling with a problem before they give up. You need to give an indication of the maximum time it is worth devoting to such a problem, but make sure this is fairly generous or you will encourage learners to give up before they have really exhausted all their skill and ingenuity. If you have other media components in your pack- age you will need to do similar estimates of the time needed for the work involved there, and don't forget the time learners may need for doing their *continuous assessment assignments* and any preparation for tutorials and anything else you or the system are expecting of them.

If after making the best estimate you can, you find that you have more than 60 hours work for a supposedly 40-hour course, you have no alternative but to rethink it and slim it down considerably. Having effectively to rewrite your materials is often painful and always additional work. You can help to lighten your own workload by keeping a careful check on the workload you are creating for you learners.

wrap-around is the term used to describe a course or package of self-instructional material which is created by wrapping the teaching elements around existing material. There may be suitable textbooks, technical manuals, journal articles, *video* or *audio* tapes, practical kits and *computer-assisted learning* packages in existence which would very competently supply the content of your package. You can then write a *study guide* or *workbook* to wrap around them and supply the additional elements which would create an open or distance learning package.

In addition to the usual elements in a course or study guide you might need to add further explanations, contrasting opinions, alternative or more relevant examples or case studies, *questions* and *activities* with *feedback*, *assignments*, *illustrations*, *summaries*, a *glossary*, some cross-referencing and an *index*. If you are wrapping around print you might want to add other *media*.

This procedure saves time and financial resources but you need to be careful about *copyright*. You can buy the items and provide them in your package, or expect the learners to buy them. You can negotiate the use of various items and pay for copyright permission. Overall this can still be less expensive than producing yourself all the material you need from scratch.

Where to find out more

These are a few starting points for learning more about the possibilities and practices of open and distance learning from current research in the field to catalogues of self-instructional materials for sale.

Organizations

In the distance learning arena:

International Centre for Distance Learning (ICDL), The Open University, Milton Keynes.
   This is a documentation centre on worldwide distance education with constantly up-dated details of courses, programmes (around 14,000 currently), institutions and the literature of distance education. The database is available on-line and on CD-ROM.

There are a number of international collaborative groups such as:
European Association of Distance Teaching Universities (EADTU).
European Distance Education Network (EDEN).
International Council for Distance Education (ICDE).
Asian Association of Open Universities (AAOU).

More concerned with open learning:
British Association for Open Learning, 15 Hitchin Street, Baldock, Herts SG7 6AL.
International Extension College, Office D, Dale's Brewery, Gwydir Street, Cambridge CB1 2LJ.
National Council for Educational Technology, Sir William Lyons Road, Science Park, University of Warwick, Coventry CV4 7EZ.
National Extension College, 18 Brooklands Avenue, Cambridge CB2 2HN.

National Open Learning Library (*for inspection not borrowing*),
Birmingham Open Learning Development Unit (BOLDU), Unit 1, Holt
Court (South), Aston Science Park, Birmingham B7 4EG.
Open College, FREEPOST, Warrington, WA2 7BR.
Open Learning Federation, 41, Edgely Road, Countesthorpe, Leicester LE8 3QN.
Open Learning Foundation, Angel Gate, City Road, London EC1 2RS.
Open University, Walton Hall, Milton Keynes MK7 6AA.
Scottish Council for Educational Technology, 74 Victoria Crescent Road,
Glasgow G12 9JN.
Training, Enterprise and Education Directorate (TEED), Department of
Employment, St. Mary's House, Moorfoot, Sheffield S1 4PQ.

Courses and packages

You can find a wide variety of courses in open and distance learning, both
short and long, professional or academic, and offered by a wide spectrum of
organizations. For example, there are courses offered by SCOTVEC in
Scotland and by RSA and City and Guilds in the rest of the UK, under the
auspices of the 'Scheme of Awards in the Development and Delivery of
Flexible and Open Learning' (ADDFOL). The Open University, UK, and
the International Extension College run courses, as does the Association of
European Correspondence Schools. Some universities offer postgraduate
diplomas and masters degrees in the field of distance education. Many of
these courses are available 'at a distance'.

There are also open learning packages to help you come to grips with
every aspect of open learning. A reasonably comprehensive series of packs is
the 'Developing Good Practice in Open Learning' series produced for the
Employment Department through its Training Agency (now TEED).

Books

There is a wealth of literature on specific aspects of open and distance learning.
These are some recent books.

Bates, AW (ed.) (1990) *Media and Technology in European Distance Education*,
Milton Keynes: EADTU and the Open University.

Bosworth, D (1991) *Open Learning*, London: Cassell.

Dixon, K (1987) *Implementing Open Learning in Local Authority Institutions*, London: Further Education Unit.

Eraut, M et al (eds) (1991) *Flexible Learning in Schools*, Sheffield: Employment Department.

Evans, T and Nation, D (eds) (1989) *Critical Reflections on Distance Education*, London: Falmer Press.

Harris, D (1987) *Openness and Closure in Distance Education*, London: Falmer Press.

Hodgson, V, Mann, S and Snell, R (eds) (1987) *Beyond Distance Teaching – Towards Open Learning*, Buckingham: SRHE and Open University Press.

Jones, A, Kirkup, G and Kirkwood, A (1992) *Personal Computers for Distance Education*, London: Paul Chapman.

Keegan, D (1990) *Foundations of Distance Education* (2nd edn), London: Routledge.

Mason, R and Kaye, A (eds) (1989) *Mindweave: Communication, Computers and Distance Education*, Oxford: Pergamon.

Paine, N (ed.) (1988) *Open Learning in Transition*, London: Kogan Page in association with the National Extension College.

Parer, M (ed.) (1989) *Development, Design and Distance Education*, Churchill, Victoria Centre for Distance Learning, Gippsland Institute of Advanced Education.

Race, P (1989) *The Open Learning Handbook*, London: Kogan Page.

Robinson, K (ed.) (1989) *Open and Distance Learning for Nurses*, Harlow: Longman.

Rowntree, D (1990) *Teaching through Self-instruction*, London: Kogan Page.

Rumble, G and Oliveira, J (eds) (1992) *Vocational Education at a Distance: International Perspectives*, London: Kogan Page.

Temple, H (1991) *Open Learning in Industry*, Harlow: Longman.

Thorpe, M (1988) *Evaluating Open and Distance Learning*, Harlow: Longman.

Thorpe, M and Grugeon, D (eds) (1987) *Open Learning for Adults*, Harlow: Longman.

TVEI (1991) *Flexible Learning: A Framework for Education and Training in the Skills Decade*, Sheffield: TVEI Unit, Employment Department.

Udace (1990) *Open College Networks and National Vocational Qualifications*, Leicester: NIACE.

And all the other books in Kogan Page's Open and Distance Learning Series.

Periodicals

American Journal of Distance Education (Pennsylvania State University).
Bulletin of the International Council for Distance Education (Norway: ICDE).
Educational Technology and Training International (London: Kogan Page).
Distance Education (University of South Queensland, Australia).
Journal of Distance Education (Athabasca University, Canada).
Open Learning (Harlow: Longman).
Supported Self-Study (Coventry: NCET).

Also published annually is the *Open Learning Directory* (Oxford: Pergamon) which contains details of some 2,000 or more open learning packages in professional and vocational training along with current information about package developers, support or delivery centres, and other open learning organizations.

References

Coffey, J (1988) 'The open learning movement' (guest editorial), *Programmed Learning and Educational Technology*, **25** 3, 195–6.

Gagné, Robert, M (1975) The Conditions of Learning (2nd edn) London: Holt, Rinehart and Winston.

Holt, D and Bonnici, J (1988) 'Learning to manage through open learning: a case study in international collaboration', *Programmed Learning and Educational Technology*, **25** 3, 245–57.

Jack, M (1988) 'The Strathclyde open learning experiment', *Open Learning*, **3** 1, 52.

Kaye, A (1989) 'Computer-mediated communication in distance education', in Mason, R and Kaye, A (eds), *Mindweave: Communication, Computers and Distance Education*, Oxford: Pergamon.

Keegan, D (1990) *Foundations of Distance Education*, London: Routledge.

Lewis, R and Spencer, D (1986) *What is Open Learning?*, London: Council for Educational Technology.

Lockwood, F (1992) *Activities in Self-Instructional Texts*, London: Kogan Page.

National Council for Educational Technology (1990) *Open and Flexible Learning Information Pack*, Coventry: NCET.

Paine, N (ed.) (1989) *Open Learning in Transition: An Agenda for Action*, London: Kogan Page with the National Extension College.

Perry, W and Rumble, G (1987) *A Short Guide to Distance Education*, Cambridge: International Extension College.

Rowntree, D (1992) *Exploring Open and Distance Learning*, London: Kogan Page.